Virtual Communication: Another Form of Communication?

Remus RUNCAN

ISBN: 978-165-50-7753-1

DEDICATION

I dedicate this book to my wife, Patricia, and our teenage daughters –
Alessia and Gloria – who were there for me. They understood the risks
and resisted the pressure of being part of these relatively newly emerging
virtual social networks.

TABLE OF CONTENTS

Foreword

Though not stated as such, the main goal of Remus Runcan's book titled ***Virtual Communication: Another Form of Communication?*** is to analyse the **risks of virtual communication**, a form of communication that has most properties, the appearance, the essence, and the effect of **communication** without being **communication**.

To do so, the author had to identify possible negative external and internal conditions, events or situations in virtual communication; to determine causal relationships between probable hindrances, their magnitude and likely outcomes of virtual communication; to evaluate various outcomes of under different assumptions and probabilities that each outcome will take place in virtual communication; to apply qualitative and quantitative techniques to reduce outcome uncertainty and associated human costs, liabilities and losses in virtual communication.

The author did so by tackling the most important aspects of **(virtual) communication** from a sociological perspective.

Possible negative external and internal conditions, events or situations in virtual communication are identified through a thorough analysis of the **need for communication**. The author analyses physiological, social, identity, affective, and spiritual needs in an attempt to explain the increasing addiction to virtual communication among our contemporaries. In the same context, the author presents the main **forms of communication** from the perspective of the way messages are coded and conveyed, as well as the **levels of**

communication, showing that virtual communication has come to cover interpersonal, group, public, and mass communication.

This is a good opportunity for the author to determine the cause-and-effect relationships between people and Divinity, between friends, between husband and wife, between parents and children, and between professionals at the workplace, relationships that can lead to both understanding and misunderstanding, to communication and miscommunication.

Communication outcomes are evaluated from the perspective of social, cultural, psychological, and physical **barriers to communication**

The author applies qualitative (narration) and quantitative (demographics) techniques in an attempt to demonstrate that the **communication risks** associated to virtual communication are considerable in terms of costs, liabilities and losses. He analyses the relationship between communication and lie and between communication and manipulation, reaching the conclusion that virtual communication should not replace face-to-face communication.

Remus Runcan's book is not a premiere in the field, but it adds a new dimension to research in the field of virtual communication: the spiritual dimension.

Georgeta Raţă

Introduction

Communication has been the topic that has benefited from the particular attention of numerous valuable researchers during the 20th century and at the beginning of the 21st century. This is due to several reasons, among which the large number of forms of communication and their omnipresence in all social processes.

"Communication is essential in the functioning of any society given that communicational processes carry social structures and cultural models. It can be seen as a functional premise necessary in any social system and as a basic social process in itself." (Sachelarie and Petrescu, 2006, 10)

Though, given that the development of media of communications allows people to communicate more than ever (they can rely on several channels of communication), we should try and see whether the process of communication has known a deep development or it has only engendered dilution of the essence by emphasising the amount and not the quality of the communication process!

Are we turning more profound in communication, more empathic, more united? Are family relationships stronger, or is everything more superficial, more tiresome or even manipulator?! Does this type of communication lead to some kind of dangerous addiction?! These are questions that more and more specialists and participants to the process of communication ask in this communication context where people no longer communicate because they live but live to communicate!

As Roman Jakobson stated in Bougnoux (2000, 31), communication has a phatic function, i.e. it allows contact and establishing relationships. The value of communication resides in both its informational and relational components. We need to correlate, in the process of communication, to correlate increase of information and deepening of relationships; otherwise, we risk wasting our time and making noise instead of communicating true messages.

This chapter aims at approaching the issue of communication starting from the definitions of the concept and at reaching the concept of virtual communication. We detail the human need for communication, the types of communication, the levels of communication, the barriers to communication, the impact of communication on human relationships and, finally, a few risks in virtual communication.

1. Communication: A Sociological Perspective

1.1. Communication: Definitions

The term communication comes from the Latin *communis/communicatio* meaning "to put together, to relate to, to share something with somebody". Communication is a study area for sociologists, psychologists, semioticians, linguists, politologists, IT specialists, philosophers, theologians, anthropologists, and, more recently, mass media specialists.

This is the reason why it is very difficult to define communication: it is such a vast domain, that it is very rare to find, in literature, two similar definitions of communication. In fact, all social and humane sciences see communication as a means of sharing information, impressions, scientific discoveries, etc. Without communication, no matter its form, there is no education – this is why communication is vital for the progress of humankind.

Paul Watzlawick's *five axioms of communication* (Watzlawick, Beavin-Bavelas and Jackson, 1967) still apply to communication and synthesise the main aspects tackled in this book:

Axiom 1: "One cannot not communicate."

Axiom 2: "Every communication has a content and relationship aspect such that the latter classifies the former and is therefore a meta-communication."

Axiom 3: "The nature of a relationship is dependent on the punctuation of the partners' communication procedures."

Axiom 4: "Human communication involves both digital and analogic modalities."

Axiom 5: "Inter-human communication procedures are either symmetric or complementary, depending on whether the relationship of the partners is based on differences or parity."

It is true that humans communicate even when he refuses to do it! Humans communicate indifference, madness, isolation, disappointment, etc. one does not necessarily need words for communication actually happens. "Even when you say nothing, you manage to say something. Accelerated respiration, reddening or whitening cheeks, perspiration [...] all these signs communicate something, therefore they are communication components." (Nuţă, 2004, 12) In addition, humans communicate even when they refuse to do it. Watzlawick and his team from the School of Palo Alto also stated that communication is simultaneous, communication is continuous, humans use two ways of communicating (digital and analogic), communication is irreversible, communication is symmetrical or complementary, and communication involves accommodation and adaptation (Nuţă, 2004, 12-20).

1.1.1. Communication: General Definitions

Abraham Moles defined communication taking into account only what is general in all communication acts, independently of the particular nature of the signs used: the elementary act of communication implies the existence of an sender that extracts, from a repertoire, a certain number of signs that he assembles according to certain laws; of a channel through which the message is transferred in space and time; and finally a receiver that receives the ensemble of signs constituting the message, identifies them with the signs he has in his own repertoire and then, after assembling them, he perceives forms, regularities, meanings that he eventually stores in his memory, subjected, more or less, to the laws of for oblivion. (Moles, 1974, 140)

This definition is of great value: it is rather general and it covers all communication acts; it starts from the premise that both sender and receiver have similar perceptions, at least partially, for the communication act to take place.

"Communication is the process of emitting a message and transmitting it in a coded way through a channel to a recipient to be received." (Zamfir and Vlăsceanu, 1998, 123)

According to this definition, humans communicate ever since they are born: the first cry of a newly-born says, in an original way, that he/she is born and needs attention. Even in his/her intra-uterine life, a baby communicates non-verbally by moving his/her arms and legs: we fail to always decipher the codes.

In 1948, Lasswell synthesised the steps of communication and suggested the following communication model: Who says what/along what channel/to whom and with what effect? (O'Sullivan et al., 2001, 74)

"Communication is a social phenomenon implying both intent to emit and intent to receive a message. Communication cannot be 'private'; it cannot subsume the behaviours of isolated individuals but the actions of individuals that have, in a semiologic context, social relationships with their pairs." (Fârte, 2004, 19)

Communication occurs at both cognitive and affective and behavioural levels.

Pierre Guiraud defined communication, back in 1963, as "[...] the transfer of information through messages." (Guiraud, 1963, in Haineş, 1998, 9)

In 1970, Frank Dance, in a reference article, scanned almost everything written about communication until that year and found 30 key terms defining communication, terms that he grouped into 15 conceptual groups as below (Dance, 1970, 204-208):

1. Symbols/Verbal/Speech

"Communication is the verbal interchange of thought or idea." (J. B. Hoben, 1954, 77)

2. Understanding

"Communication is the process by which we understand others and in turn endeavour to be understood by them. It is dynamic, constantly changing and shifting in response to the total situation." (M. P. Andersen, 1959)

3. Interaction/Relationship/Social Process

"Interaction, even on the biological level, is a kind of communication; otherwise common acts could not occur." (G. H. Mead, 1963, 107)

4. Reduction of Uncertainty

"Communication arises out of the need to reduce uncertainty, to act effectively, to defend or strengthen the ego" (D. C. Barnlund, 1964, 200)

5. *Process*

"Communication: the transmission of information, ideas, emotions, skills, etc., by the use of symbols-words, pictures, figures, graphs, etc. It is the act or process of transmission that is usually called communication." (B. Belerson and G. A. Steiner, 1964, 254)

6. *Transfer/Transmission/Interchange*

"[...] the connecting thread appears to be the idea of something's being transferred from one thing, or person, to another. We use the word "communication" sometimes to refer to what is so transferred, sometimes to the means, by which it is transferred, sometimes to the whole process. In many cases, what is transferred in this way continues to be shared; if I convey information to another person, it does not leave my own possession through coming into his. Accordingly, the word 'communication' acquires also the sense of participation. It is in this sense, for example, that religious worshipers are said to communicate." (A. J. Ayer, 1955, 12)

7. *Linking/Biding*

"Communication is the process that links discontinuous parts of the living world to one another." (J. Ruesch, 1957, 462)

8. *Communality*

"It (communication) is a process that makes common to two or several what was the monopoly of one or some." (A. Gode, 1959)

9. Channel/Carrier/Means/Route

"[...] the means of sending military messages, orders, *etc.* as by telephone, telegraph, radio, couriers." (The American College Dictionary, 1964, 244)

10. Replicating Memories

"Communication is the process of conducting the attention of another person for the purpose of replicating memories." (F. A. Cartier and K. A. Harwood, 1953, 73)

11.   Discriminative   Response/Behaviour Modifying/Response/Change

"Communication is the discriminatory response of an organism to a stimulus." (S. S. Stevens, 1950, 689)

"So, communication between two animals is said to occur when one animal produces a chemical or physical change in the environment (signal) that influences the behaviour of another [...]." (H. Frings, 1967, 297)

12. Stimuli

"Every communication act is viewed as a transmission of information, consisting of discriminative stimuli, from a source to a recipient." (T. M. Newcomb, 1966, 66)

13. Intentional

"In the main, communication has as its central interest those behavioural situations in which a source transmits a message to a receiver(s) *with conscious intent to affect the latter's behaviours.*" (G. A. Miller, 1966, 92)

14. Time/Situation

"The communication process is one of transition from one structured situation-as-a-whole to another, in preferred design." (B. Sondel, 1956, 148)

15. Power

"[...] communication is the mechanism by which power is exerted." (S. Schacter, 1951, 191)

1.1.2. Virtual Communication: Definitions

Communication has all these features and more, developed after information technology established itself in the second half of the 20th century. The end of the 20th century and the beginning of the 21st century brought about Internet networks that enriched the meaning of communication by launching the cyber-space where people communicate intensely and confront with numerous opportunities and risks: this challenged communication theoreticians to define the concept of *virtual communication*.

Given the large number of definitions and their diversity (engendered by the forms of communication that use technological discoveries), we need to admit that the idea of a science of communication is, for the moment, precariously fundamental (McQuail, 1999, 237). Monitoring the interest in this field in many scientific fields, we can assist at the crystallisation of the concept of communication in times when it becomes more and more *virtual*.

Language dictionaries define the word *virtual* as follows: "1. Existing or resulting in essence or effect though not in actual fact, form, or name: *the virtual extinction of the buffalo.* 2. Existing in the mind, especially as a product of the imagination. Used in literary criticism of a text. 3. *Computers* Created, simulated, or carried on by means of a computer or computer network: *virtual conversations in a chatroom."* (*The American Heritage Dictionary of the English Language.* Online: http://www.yourdictionary.com/virtual#americanheritage)

Communication needs to be redefined in a digitalised era. With the development of the Internet, communication becomes more and more virtual, covering much of the space of face-to-face communication in auditoria or churches long time ago.

In everything that follows, we use the phrase *virtual communication* based on our own definition rooted in both classical definitions of the term *communication* and in the meaning of the term *virtual.*

Virtual communication is a form of communication that implies the existence of a sender, a coded message and a receiver. The difference between *virtual communication* and *face-to-face communication* lies in the type of message coding: virtual communication is coded analogically or, in most cases, digitally, and it is transmitted long-distance (no matter how far), in real time and through technologies (telegraph, telephone, Internet, etc.).

The term *virtual* is not used as an antonym for the term *real* (a meaning specific to philosophy), but bearing the meaning it has in physics.

Virtual communication overpasses the traditional meaning of communication and acquires new meanings involving both fantastic opportunities and equivalent risks. The issue here is that of the capacity of decoding messages: what matters is that communication be efficient and not just another form of communication.

Virtual communication is that type of communication mediated by the new information technologies through short message service (sms), socialisation networks, e-mail, chat, video conferencing, etc. Geographical distance and delays are no longer impediments in communication: it is almost instantaneous. The main attraction of this new type of communication is that one can participate actively in the debates. *Virtual communication* tends to spread more and more, covering a space which sued to be covered, in the past, by *face-to-face communication*. "Virtual culture based on integrated information technology allows the building up of another society, of a cyber-society." (Lemeni, *Cultura virtuală – expresie a unei false comunicări.* Online: http://www.crestinortodox.ro/religie/cultura-virtuala-expresie-unei-false-comunicari-118483.html)

Bob Dignen, after organising a conference on virtual communication, concluded that, "During the conference I went to, which looked mainly at the challenges facing international teams, there seemed to be a shared assumption that virtual communication was a poor cousin of face-to-face. And the fact that people working in international teams had to communicate virtually became a de facto explanation (or at least one important explanation) of why these teams seemed to underperform regularly. But I'm not so sure." (Dignen, *Teaching virtual communication skills.* Online: http://peo.cambridge.org/index.php?option=com_content&view=arti cle&id=189:teaching-virtual-communication-skills-by-bob-dignan&catid=3:blog&Itemid=2). We agree with this points of view because *virtual communication* is somehow restricted, i.e. there is no non-verbal communication or paralanguage in it.

The effects of virtual communication are difficult to anticipate; this is why, in this book, besides a general analysis of communication, we also aim at identifying the possible specific effects that *virtual communication* has on human relationships. Adrian Lemeni noticed,

> "In real society, communication aims at achieving communion; it is a way and an expression of communion, it is more than just mere information. In communication, a word is not only information; it is also the presence of somebody in words that can be turned into acts. It is not information, but the overwhelming presence of a person that makes communication more authentic. True communication occurs when we are in what we say; a word's authority is acquired when there is no exteriority and discrepancy between what we say and what we live." (Lemeni, *Cultura virtuală – expresie a unei false comunicări.* Online: http://www.crestinortodox.ro/religie/cultura-virtuala-expresie-unei-false-comunicari-118483.html).

The supporters of such a type of communication admit that, though not perfect, *virtual communication* is evolving: "Effective virtual communication is an evolutionary process that requires constant adjustment based on current global trends and technology. What may be considered effective today may not be as effective in the future. As technology advances, so does virtual communication. For example, when email was first introduced to the public, it was used primarily for personal use. As the business world noticed its effectiveness and capabilities, new advancements in email, such as cell phone access or email advertisements, became the norm." (Papa, *Effective Virtual Communication.* Online: http://www.ehow.com/about_6756180_effective-virtualcommunication.html#page=0).

In parallel with *virtual communication*, other concepts emerge and evolve in the social sciences (anthropology, communication science, media and social psychology, political science, sociology), such as *visual competence* (with its four dimensions – visual production, perception, interpretation and reception competencies) – both of them engendered by the processes of globalisation and digitalisation (Müller, 2008).

Communication has also been defined as **shared meaning**. Tom D. Daniels and Barry K. Spiker (1987, 23) define **communication** as "shared meaning created among two or more people through verbal and nonverbal transaction".

One additional mention should be made about this definition: **meaning** only occurs when **information** – the basic raw material of communication, which includes any aspect of the environment in which one can discern a pattern – is placed within a context.

Communication also may be modelled in various ways.

According to the authors mentioned above (Daniels and Spiker, 1987, 36), there are three ***models of communication as shared meaning*** that provide different descriptions of the process of communication both in everyday life and in organisational life: *linear, interactional*, and *transactional*. No matter the model, knowing and properly understanding them could help a manager to better understand the way things work in his or her firm, the causes of both success and failure, and to make the right decisions to improve its activity.

Linear models provide the simplest description of the communication process: they represent **communication** as the *one-way flow of a message from a source to a receiver*. Thus, David K. Berlo (in Daniels and Spiker, 1987, 36) developed a model of communication that reflects the linear view: in his model, a Source transmits a Message through a Channel to a Receiver (see Table 1.1 below).

Table 1.1. Berlo's linear model of communication (after Daniels and Spiker, 1987, 36)

Source	Message	Channel	Receiver
Communication Skills	Elements	Seeing	Communication Skills
Attitudes	Structure	Hearing	Attitude
Knowledge	Content	Touching	Knowledge
Social System	Treatment	Smelling	Social System
Culture	Code	Tasting	Culture

Their own attitudes, prior knowledge, socio-cultural background, and other factors in this process affect both the Source and the Receiver.

The Source must encode (change ideas into symbols – verbal and nonverbal stimuli that are assumed to have common referents for the Source and Receiver) the Message; the Receiver must decode it (assign meaning to symbols).

The Message is transmitted through a Channel that might involve speech, writing, or some system of nonverbal gestures.

Fidelity of the Message may be affected by Noise (anything that interferes with or distorts the message, as it is transmitted through the Channel). Message fidelity refers to more than the simple clarity or quality of transmission: it is linked with the idea of obtaining a desired response. Therefore, Noise should be understood as anything that interferes with the process of obtaining this response: a Receiver's communication skill, attitudes, knowledge, cultural background, and social position are potential sources of Noise.

Interactional models improve the understanding of these dynamics because they emphasise a *two-way perspective of communication*:

This model portrays communication as a process of Message exchange: Person A (Source) sends a Message to Person B (Receiver) who becomes a Source responding with a Message to Person A, who is now the Receiver: the participants in communication exchange roles during the process. Daniels and Spiker (1987, 36) advanced their own interactional model of communication (see Table 1.2 below).

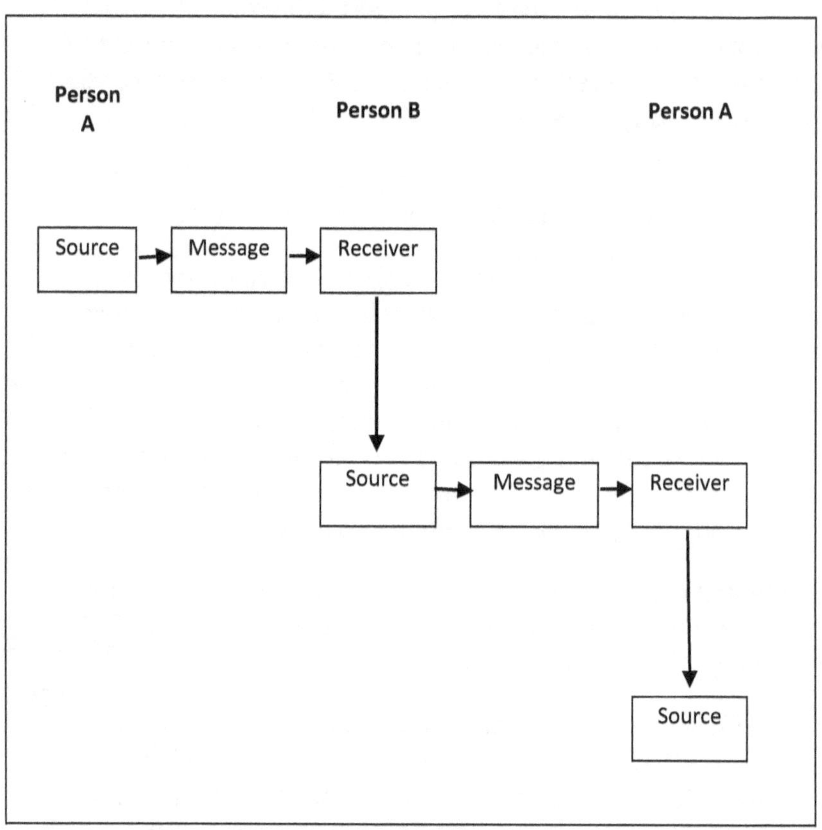

Transactional models emphasise the idea that *communication is mutual as well as reciprocal.* For J. Wenberg and W. Wilmot (in Daniels and Spiker, 1987, 38), all persons are engaged in sending (encoding) and receiving (decoding) messages simultaneously: each person is constantly sharing in the encoding and decoding process and each person is affecting the other. In this case communication occurs without sharp distinctions between Source and Receiver roles: a person occupies both roles at the same time (see Table 1.3 below).

Table 1.3. Wenberg and Wilmot's transactional model of communication (after Daniels and Spiker, 1987, 38)

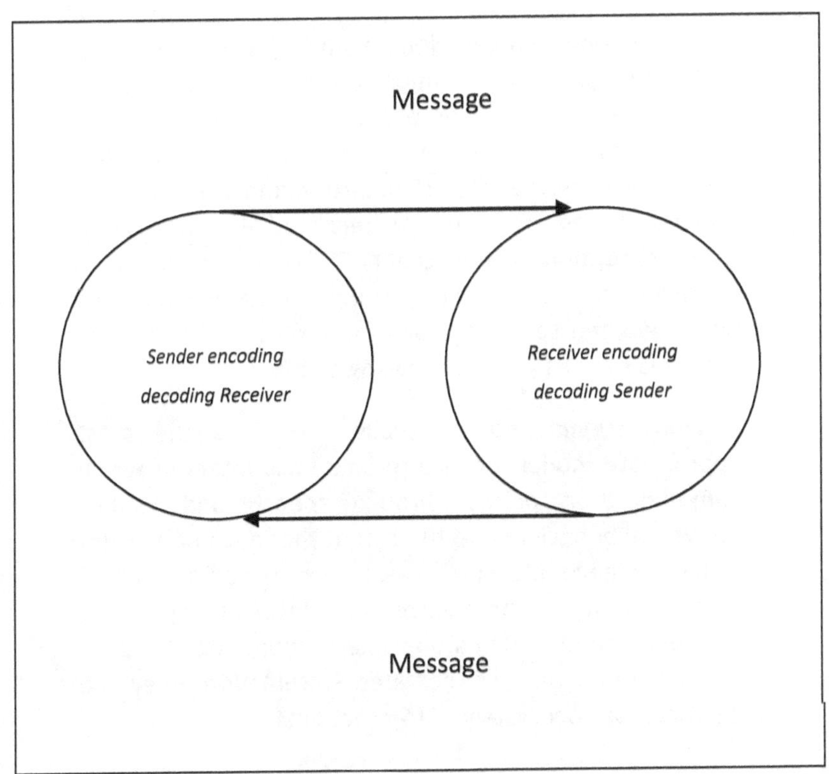

Linear, *interactional* and *transactional models* all can be applied as accurate *descriptions of the communication process*, but their ranges of application differ:

- A **linear model** is very limited because few instances of human communication truly occur in a one-way fashion: thus, episodes of superior giving orders to subordinates and some forms of public communication (issuing policy pronouncements through memoranda or newsletters with no expectation of feedback) appear to be linear.

- An **interactional model** does a good job of describing mediated forms of communication: thus, interaction through an electronic or paper medium (e.g., letters, memoranda, or computer terminals) separates the communicators and often structures communication as a process of message exchange (tele-mediated interaction is an exception if the channel allows simultaneous, bidirectional message flow – e.g., in teleconferences when you can see and hear others on visual and voice channels even as you are speaking to them);

- A **transactional model** usually serves as the most appropriate model for face-to-face encounters in which communication occurs through speech and various nonverbal behaviours, to the extent that each participant in such an encounter has an awareness of self and others in the situation, the Source and Receiver aspects of human communication are enacted simultaneously: thus, some forms of tele-mediated interaction may be characterised accurately as transactional.

Not everyone is prepared to define **communication as shared meaning**. Three other definitions of **communication** are applied frequently in the organisational setting: *source experience, receiver experience,* and *bilateral experience.*

Berelson and Steiner (in Daniels and Spiker, 1987, 35) define **communication** as *"the transmission of information, ideas, emotions, skills, etc., by the use of symbols"*, as an act of message (symbolic content in spoken or written form) transmission performed by a source. Source experience definitions of communication say nothing about what happens when messages and information are received (if they are understood, if the receiver's interpretation is the same as the source's interpretation, etc.). Or, it is obvious that the events that occur when receiving a message may determine the ***effectiveness of communication***.

There are two versions of the **receiver experience**: *passive,* and *active.* In the *passive* version (according to which humans respond passively to stimuli), **communication** is defined as "the discriminatory response of an organism to a stimulus" (S. S. Stevens, in Daniels and Spiker, 1987, 35). In the *active* version, **communication** occurs whenever a person actively interprets another person's verbal and nonverbal behaviours by selecting information, assigning meanings, and making inferences and choices (S. W. Littlejohn, *idem*). Receiver experience definitions of communication say nothing about what happens when messages and information are transmitted.

G. A. Sanborn (in Daniels and Spiker, 1987, 36) define **communication** as "the process of sending and receiving messages", a process in which the source must transmit "meaningful signals" in a message, and a receiver must perceive and assign meaning to the message. This definition says nothing about the fact that meaning must be shared for **communication** to occur. Though, this approach –

that treats messages as concrete objects and effectiveness as a problem of getting a desired response – has been the most commonly used in **organisational communication**, especially in the traditional functionalist perspective.

1.2 Elements of Communication

Despite the large number of definitions of communication and of the vast areas they cover, we should not fall into the dangerous extreme of considering that everything is communication in our world. This is why we try, below, to establish a few components of human communication alone.

There are a few major dimensions of communication labelled in different ways by different authors:

- *Message* (the things that are communicated);

- *Source / emisor / sender / encoder* (the entity who encodes the message);

- *Form* (the form in which is sent the message);

- *Channel* (the medium through which is sent the message);

- *Destination / receiver / target / decoder* (the entity to whom is sent the message);

- *Effect / impact* (desired or undesired, of the message sent)

Hence, the several ways of decomposing communication, from the simplest to the most complex ones.

Shannon and Weaver's first model of communication (1949, 188) – also called linear model of communication – consisted of three primary parts – sender, message and receiver (Figure 1.1). In this model, there is no feedback for a continuous exchange of information, and there is no mention of "noise".

Figure 1.1 Shannon and Weaver's first model of communication

Later on, Shannon and Weaver structured their model based on the elements below:

- An *information source*, which produces a message;

- A *transmitter*, which encodes the message into signals;

- A *channel*, to which signals are adapted for transmission;

- A *receiver*, which "decodes" (i.e., reconstructs) the message from the signal;

- A *destination*, where the message arrives.

Wilbur Schramm indicated, in 1954, that we should also examine the (un)desired effect/impact that a message has on the receiver (Figure 1.2)

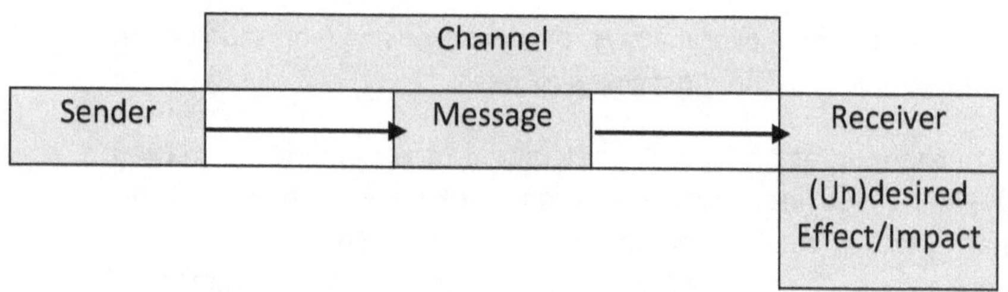

Figure 1.3 Schramm's model of communication

David Berlo expanded Shannon and Weaver's model of communication creating, in 1960, the Source – Message – Channel – Receiver Model of Communication (Figure 1.3):

S		M		C		R
Communication skills		Content		Hearing		Communication skills
Attitude		Elements		Seeing		Attitude
Knowledge		Treatment		Touching		Knowledge
Social system		Structure		Tasting		Social system
Culture		Codes		Feeling		Culture

Figure 1.3 Berlo's model of communication

In 1970, Barnlund proposed a transactional model of communication in which the source and the receiver are simultaneously engaging in the sending and receiving of messages (Figure 1.4):

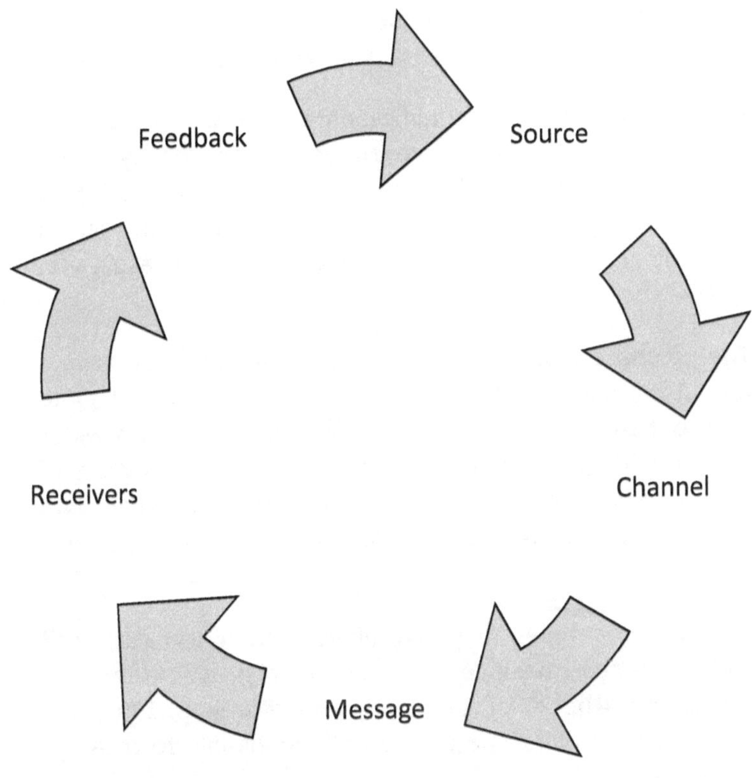

Figure 1.4 Barnlund's transactional model of communication

The model that better serves the goal of this book is the one advanced by Denis McQuail. He identified five components of communication – communicator, message, code, communication means, and receiver capable of decoding the message. In all this, he started from a few suppositions: there is rationality, intentionality in communication, there is a linear perspective on communication, and communication always starts with a transmitter. (McQuail, 1999, 29)

The first element of communication according to McQuail is the *communicator* (also called *sender* or *transmitter* by other authors). There is no communication without a communicator. A communicator can be a person, a group, an organisation, a newspaper, a blog, a Facebook page, a profile on a matchmaking site, or a *second life* site.

The second element is the *message*. Communication always has content; it is about something or someone. It can be about some information, but the term message is preferred because it is wider and has a more complex semantics. A message is "an ensemble of symbols configured around an idea, transferred between two milestones capable of using a compatible system of codes." (Nadolu, 2007, 18)

At the same time, there is subjectivity in the receiver's interpretation of the message because what is a message to somebody can be a noise for somebody else (McQuail, 1999, 31). Sometimes, noise "can alter a message until impossible to receive." (Ritt, 2004, 14)

The third element is a *code*. To reach a receiver, a message needs to be coded in such a way that the receiver be able to decode it to understand it. Linguistic or social, a code system needs to be the same for both the sender and the receiver. If the sender codes the message in English and the receiver decodes it Romanian, for instance, communication is inefficient. The same occurs when we encode a message and transmit it to a deaf person. Code compatibility can range within 0% and 100%: extremes are impossible to reach – 0% communication does not exist in practice, and 100%

communication cannot be reached because there is no perfect communication in interpersonal relationships. "A code represents a special set of rules that translates a paradigm into another." (Ritt, 2004, 14) How we perceive meanings is a matter of semiotics and it is not the goal of this book to talk about signs, concepts, objects, etc.!

The fourth element is the *communication means*. A communication means is any possible form of capturing somebody's attention and of making one's messages available for anybody else – through speaking, writing, the use of electronic means, movies, sculpture, painting (McQuail, 1999, 32).

Communication means are represented by technical or physical means of converting a message into a signal capable of being transmitted through a channel. (Fiske, 2003, 35) According to John Fiske (Fiske, 35, 35-36), communication means can be grouped into three main categories:

- Presentational communication means: voice, face, and body. They are restrained to the communication instance "here" and "now".

- Representational communication means: books, paintings, photographs, writings, architecture, interior decorations, gardening, etc. They are independent from the communicator.

- Mechanical communication means: telephone, television, radio, Internet, etc.

Since the topic of this book is *virtual communication*, we can say that computer-mediated communication (sms, e-mail, socialisation networks) relies on these mechanical means developed by engineers and subjected to a high degree of risk as far as noise is concerned, which makes a message difficult to understand for the receiver.

The fifth element of communication is a *receiver*. He/she receives messages, decodes them and, in most cases, reacts. He/she is also, in many cases, an initiator, i.e. he/she responds in a certain way thus generating messages for the initiator or for the others. The *active sender – passive receiver* model occurs in learning, propaganda, and advertising, but it is not suitable for all domains. In contrast, the functional model confers the receiver an active role: he/she is no longer a receiver but a user. "The receiver's capacity of selecting and reacting determines, eventually, the choices and directions of the sender's messages." (Otovescu, 2012, 30)

The functional model seems somehow upside-down because there is greater emphasis on the receiver generating responses, initiating interpretation processes, interacting with the information, and even influencing the sender of the message.

2. The Need for Communication

It is impossible to deny the need for communication in humans! Since a child's birth, his/her parents, doctors, the extended family communicate with the child and the child learns to communicate with the other social actors.

Early experiences include speech and gesture addressed to us. In our turn, we have learned all this through practice, trial and error. But there are people who believe we are born with these basic abilities that help us learn how to speak and how to understand what we see. However, the largest part of our communication capacities need to be learned. (Agabrian, 2008, 18)

It is understood that people learn to communicate and that they develop their communication skills through practice as far as receiving messages and transmitting messages is concerned.

From the perspective of human needs, Abraham Maslow hierarchy of needs covers 5 levels of basic needs starting from the bottom (physiological needs) and up to self-actualisation needs (Figure 2.1).

After mentioning physiological needs (air, water, food; clothing and shelter; sexual competition), *safety and security needs* (personal security, financial security, health and well-being, and safety net against accidents/illness and their adverse impacts), Maslow tackles the issue of *belongingness* (friendship, intimacy, family). (Maslow, 1943, 375-378)

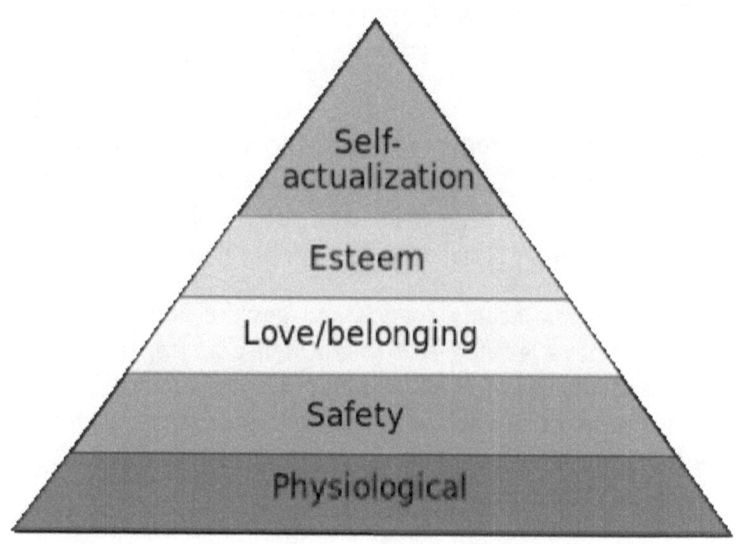

Source:http://en.wikipedia.org/wiki/Maslow%27s_hierarchy_of_nee
ds#mediaviewer/File:MaslowsHierarchyOfNeeds.svg

Figure 2.1. Maslow's hierarchy of needs represented as a pyramid with the more basic needs at the bottom

Meeting the lower levels of needs ensures the ground for higher level needs. But if the need for communication is not met, then it is impossible to feel satisfied at higher levels of needs: esteem (level 4) and self-actualisation (level 5). In 1990, other three levels were added to this pyramid, levels that also rely on communication: aesthetic needs – beauty, balance, form (level 6), development, fulfilment, happiness needs (level 7) and transcendence, contribution, supreme sense needs (level 8).

Earth's population increases each year, with Europe being an exception; the space per capita is decreasing, there is a high level of migration from isolated places toward very crowded areas, the economic development of the countries is quick – yet, paradoxically, humans are increasingly estranged, more isolated in their dwellings or offices. In this context, humans' significant need for communication is no longer met: something in them calls for help, but many people are too busy with solving problems or the problems of the others to respond efficiently to the people in need of significant social relationships!

From the point of view of its origin, the ability to communicate is a gift from God for people to be able to communicate with Him and their peers. One of the most beautiful experiences for the first humans is told in the **Bible**, where we read about the meeting of the Creator, God Himself, with His creatures, in an attempt to communicate with them. In Christian theology, communication is mentioned even before the Creation, in the description of His decision to make the man: "Let us make mankind in our image, in our likeness [...]." (Genesis 1:26). "A theology built upon revelation is deeply interested in the issue of communication because revelation is communication." (Lohisse, 2002, 18)

On the other hand, the fall of man was related to communication since the verbal exchange with a snake proved lethal for the first family. The devil asks questions, distorts concepts, and induces uncertainty – which shows that he masters the art of communication.

We evaluate below some of the human needs that explain why communication is so important starting from the premise that any human action is engendered by certain needs.

2.1 Physiological Needs

We have physiological needs – food, clothing, shelter, warmth, sleep – hence, we need to communicate. It is communication that keeps us in good health. One of the signs that betray some kind of depression is the refusal to communicate. On the other hand, if we notice some kind of danger, we need to tell others about it. If people are isolated physically, their health deteriorates little by little. In the 13th century, Emperor Frederic the II carried out an experiment to see what language children speak naturally. He took 50 newly-born children and put them in the hands of a nurse who was asked to bathe them and feed them without keeping them in her arms or speaking in their presence. All the children died before they managed to utter a word (Perry, 2002, 80). Though the experiment is tragic and unimaginable in the 21st century, it shows clearly that these physical needs are common to all humans. If we meet only these physical needs, humans cannot survive because they need significant communication.

2.2 Social Needs

Humans are, among other things, social beings, i.e. they need other people. The social status is an important element of humankind. We work not only for food and clothing; we work with other people and this is why we need social communication. One cannot imagine a factory or a company without communication.

Laurenţiu Şoitu, inspired by Wilhelm Schutz (1983), identifies three types of social needs:

- The need for inclusion as part of a certain relational system;

- The need for authority, i.e. of impacting the others;

- The need for affection, which "is sometimes subscribed to the need for respect, completes the social dimension of motivations, of communication, proving that everybody wishes to count, to represent something for the others." (Şoitu, 2001, 23)

2.3 Identity Needs

In post-modernism, after redefining the concepts of space and time, we needed to redefine the concept of identity. If, for Greek philosophers, identity was a strong one, numerical, in post-modern philosophers there is an attempt to dilute identity until complete loss. They have advanced new concepts such as multiple identities, contextual identity and, lately, they have talked about *virtual identity*. Identity is no longer seen in a strong way, but in a weak way: it relies on similarity, it is elastic, it has multiple faces and everybody can shape one's identity similar to a potter, according to one's good will and own interests. "Post-modern theories are rather reflexive and produce individual erosion, which suggests that identity can be easily reconstructed and that everybody is free to change and produce himself/herself as he/she wishes." (Fizeşan, 2010, 43)

It is extremely easy for any computer user with a connection to the Internet to create a virtual identity (because there is no legislation in the field), which allows many people to have an account or several accounts on the same socialisation network, on different networks or on *second life* sites. Because there is no control in the field, many people manage to have multiple personalities generating some kind of social schizophrenia and confusion over their identity. Such people themselves fail to know who they are!

We have, undoubtedly, identity needs and, therefore, we need to ask ourselves how identity is engendered. The way in which we communicate with other people plays a fundamental role in the shaping of our vision of ourselves (Yeung and Martin, 2003, 843).

Identity is what we are and it develops during our entire life; communication plays an essential role in this process. The people who are good communicators are also able to point out different aspects of their identity in different situations (Floyd, 2013, 27).

While we communicate, we crystallise our identity or *self* – as psychologists call it – or *ego* – as philosophers call it. The famous principle of French philosopher René Descartes – "I doubt, therefore I think; I think, therefore I am" – made numerous people ask themselves what this *ego* means and whether we can define this *ego* starting from doubt. It is difficult to believe that, starting from doubt, one can deepen the concept of identity; but it is certain that identity develops through communication, which makes the inscription on the Oracle in Delphi – "know thyself" is a necessary approach for everybody; the way to reach identity knowledge is the way of communication. We believe that this knowledge, this definition of our own identity is possible only through communication with the Creator, through communication with oneself and through validation in communication with our peers. "We acquire the knowledge of our being in the dialogue with the other(s)." (Şoitu, 2001, 22)

2.4 Affective Needs

We need family and close friends as social support and it is through communication that we can establish, maintain and deepen such relationships. These affective needs engender relationships that build up ad develop through communication. These affective needs cannot be met without significant relationships, and the latter cannot exist without communication. Happiness in family, for instance, depends on how partners, parents, children, etc. can find efficient ways of communication. To have a happy marriage is more important than income, than work status, than education, spare time or anything else from the perspective of one's satisfaction (Floyd, 2013, 27).

Tenderness and love generate satisfaction, calmness, relaxation and openness that, in turn, facilitate interpersonal communication.

These affective needs can be engendered by external factors or they can be self-initiated.

"These relationships are developed by either external factors (family, school, work), or they are self-initiated (acquaintances, friends, close friends)." (Ritt, 2004, 122)

We need to take into account that these affective needs have nothing to do with sexuality: the roots of happiness are not in sexuality (Eibl-Eibesfeldt, 1998, 141). This truth needs to be taken into account because they promote the contrary in the mass media suggesting that our affective needs are a matter of sexuality; this is but another example of manipulation, something degrading for the human being, taken to an animal level by Freud and lead by others to exacerbated erotism. This way of replacing the need for affectivity by the need to please one's sexual impulse is exacerbated by television and, increasingly, by Internet.

2.5 Spiritual Needs

Humans also need, besides what is said above, by spiritual needs because they have a spiritual component.

Kory Floyd (2013, 28) describes spirituality and distinguishes between three fields where it is manifest:

- Principles appreciated in life (I appreciate loyalty, equal treatment applied to everybody, etc.);

- People's morality, their ideas about what is good and what is bad (it is not good to steal, but if you need to lie to save somebody's life it is OK because life is more important than honesty, etc.);

- Faith and religious practices I believe in God, I believe that in life he that sows the wind shall reap the whirlwind, etc.).

Humans have spiritual needs but we think there is an even deeper need, i.e. the *need for God*; or else, one can reach spirituality without faith. We believe the following column from the Romanian newspaper *Adevărul* from April 6, 2010, is suggestive:

"Maybe the man of our days has lost the faith of his ancestors, yet he still needs spirituality.

The Protestant Church of Holland has made a historical decision: it allowed an atheist pastor who believes 'in a God that does not exist' to continue his mission. The event marks a decisive detour in the evolution of mentalities. It shows that, nowadays, God has multiple meanings depending on individuals.

Religion sociologists noted long ago that the secularisation of Western societies lead to the individualisation of religions. There are fewer and fewer Christians that accept entirely the doctrines and dogmas of the church. Each Christian establishes lone his own norms. At the same time, the decision of the Protestant Church of Holland shows, once more, that Christian institutions have lost their power. And the consequence is the increasingly wider gap between religious leaders and common believers. This is even more visible in the Catholic Church. The scandal of paedophilia in which the latter is involved shows that the trust in the Vatican is eroding. Common Catholics no longer want to be assimilated with the Vatican.

The step made by the Dutch reflects the need for spirituality of the modern world. The proof: the church of Klaas Hendrikse, the atheist pastor from Middelbourg, is full of people, which is an exception in an area characterised by the desertion of either pastors or believers. Maybe the man of our days has lost the faith of his ancestors, but he still needs spirituality.

A few years ago, French philosopher André Comte-Sponville demonstrated, in an essay, that atheists' spirituality is possible. Klaas Hendrikse shows it through his deeds and opens a new path within the Protestant Church itself. Which has understood that, in order to survive, it needs to adapt, to answer all contemporary concerns, even the most inconvenient ones." (*Nevoia de spiritualitate*. Online: http://adevarul.ro/international/in-lume/nevoia-spiritualitate-1_50ba02a77c42d5a663afa38f/index.html).

Spirituality needs to rely on communication, not on forms, on false faiths or worse, as seen in the article above, even on unfaithfulness. Here we should remind a linguistic distinction made by Constantin Noica: the existence of two related words in Romanian – *a comunica* ("to communicate") and *a cuminica* ("to give the Eucharist"). The latter "comes from the Latin *communicare* and, via religious Latin, got the same meanings in all Romance languages, i.e. 'to give/receive the Eucharist'." (Noica, 1996, 128) Spirituality is, from this perspective, communication with God. This is how our need for communication can be met.

It is interesting to note that community is also the effect of communication: "it is not without interest to note the opposed polarity of the term excommunication. This means the interdiction to give/receive Eucharist." (Nuţă, 2004, 11)

Man needs to communicate with God and he needs communion with the believers to develop and share spiritual needs.

3. Forms of Communication

Abraham Moles (1974, 140), speaking of the physical types of communication, points out the existence of two types of messages:

- Sound message, with three sub-types:

  - speech, the language of humans;

  - music, the language of sensations;

  - noise, the language of things.

- Visual message, with three sub-types:

  - the symbolic message of the printed text;

  - the message of natural or artificial forms;

  - the artistic message.

3.1 Verbal Communication

Verbal or **oral** or **spoken communication**, the most common form of communication, designates "the sharing of information between individuals by using speech" (*Verbal Communication*. Online: http://www.businessdictionary.com/definition/verbal-communication.html#ixzz3NdtXjVo5).

Despite the differences between women (who utter about 33,000 words/day) and men (who utter about 20,000 words/day), one cannot deny the importance of verbal communication in our life. (Macrae, *Sorry to interrupt, dear, but women really do talk more than men (13,000 words a day more to be precise)*. Online: http://www.dailymail.co.uk/sciencetech/article-2281891/Women-really-talk-men-13-000-words-day-precise.html) This differentiation is supported by the population pyramid of Facebook users by gender and age on January 1, 2010 below (Figure 3.1):

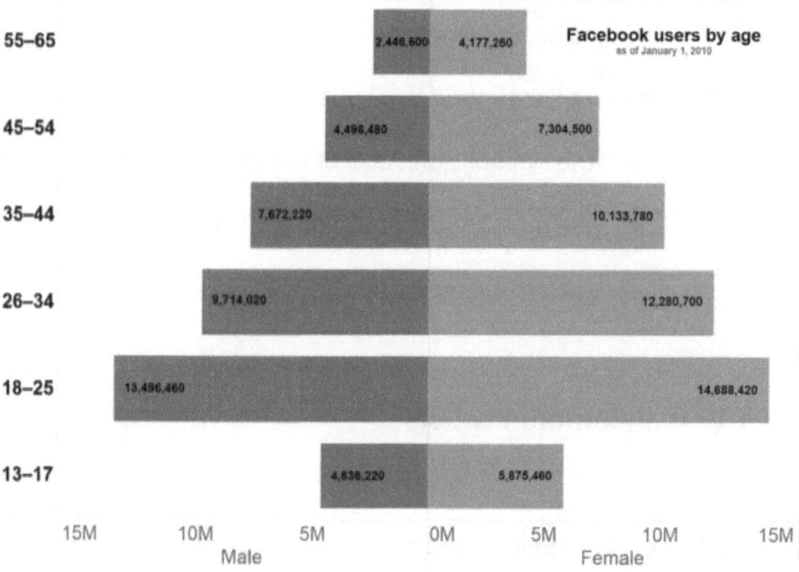

Source: http://en.wikipedia.org/wiki/Facebook

Figure 3.1 Population pyramid of Facebook users by gender and age (January 1, 2010)

"Word is the means the richest in meanings, inner prolongations and musical harmonies that we know." (Biberi, 1972, 23)

In spite of its occurrence, I will not insist too much on this type of communication because the topic of this book is *virtual communication*, which is often an alternative to verbal communication and that is gaining more and more ground in front of verbal communication. We will insist, below, on those types of communication that are either ignored or emphasised by virtual communication.

Verbal communication can be speech or conversation.

3.1.1 Speech

Speech is a monologue (there is unilateral communication from a transmitter to a receiver). The importance of this type of communication has declined compared to other historical periods (e.g., Ancient Greece and Ancient Rome).

From a sociological perspective, "speech points to the way in which a social actor uses a language and other communication resources to build up 'a point of view' or a position on what is communicated and in relation to one's interlocutors." (Beciu, 2011, 32)

Speech is sued nowadays more in the political sphere but, because it has a poor content, it is outdistanced by conversation. This deficiency, doubled by the fact that the sphere of communication has moved to the sphere of virtual, has engendered not only a speech devoid of consistency, but also the lack of appetite for listening to speeches: communication via telephone, sms, chat, socialisation networks has a much poorer vocabulary and depth of ideas.

Thus, because of superficiality, communication is increasingly difficult: pressure comes from both the sender's inability to give an intelligent speech and the receiver's inability to capture at "higher frequencies" a speech – be it on political, philosophical, religious or even social topics.

3.1.2 Conversation

In the virtual era, the form of communication the most frequent in the media, politics, education and entertainment is conversation: transmitter and receiver exchange their roles rather frequently, and interlocutors are identical and inter-changeable (Lohisse, 2002, 179).

Even on blogs and in online press, they encourage conversation on certain topics, and the readers can leave comments, points of view, in most cases monitored and benefiting from the authors' feed-back.

Conversation is possible only if the participants accept a series of principles that regulate communication, among which *cooperation*. Undoubtedly, most young people would prefer conversation detrimental to speech because of the same arguments presented under "Speech" above.

3.2 Non-verbal Communication

Non-verbal communication is a form of communication without words, i.e. "behaviour and elements of speech aside from the words themselves that transmit meaning" (*Non-verbal Communication.* Online: http://www.businessdictionary.com/definition/non-verbal-communication.html#ixzz3Ndv4JQJV) We need to remind that the first forms of communication between a mother and her child are non-verbal. It is also known as *meta-communication* (from the Greek *meta-* "beyond"), i.e. communication beyond words or "reading between the lines, understanding the meaning hidden beyond the words." (Cristescu et al., 1999, 53)

Some of its forms are silence, mimicry, gesture, touch, and emotional communication. Of all these forms, we will present only emotional communication because it is frequent in virtual communication.

Non-verbal communication is continuous, uncontrollable and unstructured.

As for the share of non-verbal communication of other forms of communication (verbal, paraverbal), a message is 55% non-verbal (gestures, mimicry, body posture, etc.), 38% voice quality (accent, punctuation, rhyme, tonality, expressivity) and only 7% words (content) (Cameron, 2005, 11). Therefore, communication is mainly non-verbal, which causes problems in virtual communication because it is computer mediated. The messages transmitted through virtual communication networks cannot communicate within the 55% range or within the 38% range (paraverbal channels). The question here is if socialisation networks provide acceptable communication to their users who wish to communicate with their friends or with complete strangers if we take into account the fact that only 7% of communication relies on written words.

In 2013, we administered a questionnaire regarding the motivation of youth to open an account or several accounts on socialisation networks. We surveyed 300 young people aged 14-30. The highest percentage of the people surveyed (38.4%) responded it was the need for communication that had pushed them to open such an account; 15.2% opened an account to be on a level with other people; 9.6%, to make more friends; 3.2%, to get more well known; 8%, for other reasons. Is such a need for communication met? Is socialisation through virtual networks satisfactory or is it merely a surrogate?

Non-verbal communication has also an emotional component. "Non-verbal channels are important in communicating feelings and attitudes." (Pânişoară, 2008, 91) This type of communication starts from the observation that we cannot transmit everything through uttered or written words. Many communication acts are related to feelings and emotions, to gestures and voice tone, with facial expressions, etc.

"Expressivity and decoding the meaning of emotions that are part of the complex process of communication are, together with speaking, writing and reading, an important way of transmitting information through specialised neuronal mechanisms in humans, located in the right hemisphere." (Răşcanu, 2007, 28)

They tried to solve this problem in virtual communication through emoticons. They aimed at transmitting the emotions of the sender through small images of the *smiley face* types. The problem is that, while emotions are natural reactions of humans in different situations, emoticons are controlled emotions (they are chosen by the user in a deliberate way): thus, emoticons may correspond or not to the user's emotions if he/she chooses to please or confuse.

The trend is to communicate emotions virtually, which leads to the risk of transmitting incomplete feelings or to communicate them improperly. A written text that transmits nothing non-verbally can be wrongfully understood or it can become a means of manipulating.

Depending on his/her personality, each individual is more or less sensitive to non-verbal indices: nervous people (anxious or introvert) are very sensitive to non-verbal communication, while delinquents or psychopaths are insensitive (Amado and Guittet, 2007, 36). This engenders increased risk for emotional people who hide behind the computer's monitor or the smart phone and, lacking non-verbal communication, can be deceived with well arranged words that generate false images; if the user is a psychopath, communication can turn lethal in a conversation with an emotional person.

Much of the **information** in **human communication** is **nonverbal behaviour** that occurs in forms other than the word symbols of a language. Gestures, for example, are considered to be a paralinguistic, constant and ubiquitous phenomenon – they do not cease when someone speaks – with a supporting role in communication. **Gesture** is defined as a "body movement that has a meaning", as a "voluntary act that belongs as such to nonverbal communication". The role of nonverbal behaviour in communication is not as clear as the role of verbal behaviour. Thus, R. Harrison (in Daniels and Spiker, 1987, 29) estimated that about 65% of the information in day-to-day interaction is nonverbal. Paul Ekman and

Wallace V. Friesen (*idem*) regarded nonverbal behaviour as "communicative" only when the person exhibiting the behaviour intends it as a message for someone else, as it may sometimes signify nothing more than random nervous system activity, without any meaning beyond its own occurrence. P. Watzlawick, J. Beavin and D. Jackson (*idem*) argued that any behaviour, be it intentional or not, is communicative if another person perceives and interprets it. Communicative or not, nonverbal behaviour can certainly influence the communication process. **Nonverbal behaviour** may be *symbolic* (it represents a referent) or *signalic* (it indicates a related event):

- ***Symbolic behaviour*** is *communicative* (e.g., nonverbal substitutes: the hitchhiker's uplifted thumb for requesting a ride, the system of hand gestures that the deaf use, the nonverbal cues that athletic coaches employ to relay plays, etc.): it depends on high-level mental processes (it is purposive and intentional).

- ***Signalic behaviour*** is *not entirely communicative* (e.g., crying indicating an intense emotional state, drooping eyelids indicating drowsiness, finger-drumming indicating annoyance, etc.).

Several forms of **nonverbal behaviour** seem to be important in **organisational communication** but only three of them – considered as very important – will be detailed below.

3.2.1. Paralanguage

Paralanguage consists of nonverbal speech sounds.

One of the most important functions of paralanguage in both spoken and written expression in organisational communication is its role in influencing person perception (his or her competence, coherence, character appeal etc.): employment interviewers' hiring decisions and judgements of an applicant's suitability for a particular type of job are influenced by accent and dialect

Tone, pitch, volume, inflection, rhythm, and *rate* are **elements of paralanguage** in *spoken expression*:

- **Tone**, "any of the musical pitches or movements in pitch that are characteristic of a given language", can indicate, for example, the type of sentence (declarative, interrogative, imperative).

- **Pitch**, the "degree of height or depth of a tone or of sound, depending upon the relative rapidity of the vibration by which it is produced", can indicate the element(s) considered of utmost importance by the speaker.

- **Volume**, the "degree of sound intensity or audibility", can indicate the speaker's superior status or self-confidence.

- **Inflection**, the "modulation of the voice; change in pitch or tone of voice", can indicate the type of sentence (declarative, interrogative) or a change in the speaker's attitude.

- **Rhythm**, the "pattern of recurrent strong and weak accents, vocalisation and silence, and the distribution and combination of these elements in speech", can indicate the speaker's level of education, his or her ethnic origin, etc.

- **Rate**, the "degree of speed", can indicate the speaker's state (calm, excited, etc.).

Paralanguage can be very important – if not essential – when the meaning of the words depends on the paralanguage elements accompanying speech.

Written expression has its own ***paralanguage elements***. Thus:

- **Tone** is marked with the help of ***punctuation marks*** (*full-stop* for a declarative sentence, *question mark* for an interrogative sentence, *exclamation mark* for an exclamatory sentence, etc.).

- **Pitch**, with the help of *italics* (for emphasis), **bold(face)** (for emphasis, headings, etc.), or <u>underlined</u> (for emphasis) words.

- **Volume**, with the help of CAPITALS and/or ***punctuation marks*** (., ?, !).

- **Inflection**, with the help of <u>underlined words</u> or of CAPITALS.

- **Rhythm**, with the help of ***punctuation marks***: *full-stop* (or *period*), *comma, colon, semicolon, question mark* (or *interrogation mark / point*), *exclamation mark* (or *exclamation point*), *quotation marks* (or *quote marks*), *brackets*, and *dash*.

- **Rate**, withthehelpofwordswrittenwithoutpauses.

3.2.2. Body Movement

Much of the information available in *face-to-face communication* is provided through **body movement**.

Ray Birdwhistell (in Daniels and Spiker, 1987, 32) claimed that all body movement is meaningful within the context in which it occurs, but other scholars questioned this idea.

There is no doubt that body movement has some important *functions in human communication*. Paul Eckman and Wallace Friesen (in Daniels and Spiker, 1987, 32; Descamps, 1989, 170-171) devised a system of gesture categories that include *emblems, illustrators,* and *regulators, affect displays,* and *adaptors*:

a) **Emblems** are *kinesics substitutes for verbal behaviour, culturally determined symbolic or coded gestures.* Though they usually are intended to transmit a particular message, their meaning may depend on the group that uses them and the context in which they occurs: the two-fingered "V" traditionally is an emblem for victory, but during the 1960s, young people also adopted it as an emblem for peace; nodding your head is almost everywhere in the world a symbol of approval, but it is a symbol of denial in Bulgaria and in Greece.

b) **Illustrators** are *culturally determined kinesic cues that directly support speech behaviour, helping to emphasise what is being said.* They include behaviours to *point out* (an object or a person with the help of the index finger), to *outline a form* (of an object with the help of the hand(s)), to *depict motion* (with the help of the hands and/or of the entire body), to *show size* (with the help of the hands), to *mark the state of mind* (by frowning one's eyebrows), etc.

c) ***Regulators*** help to *control and co-ordinate face-to-face interaction, signalling taking turn in conversations (for seeking feedback, initiating interaction, terminating conversations, etc.).* They are eye *movements* (looking at an interlocutor to give him or her the floor), *head positions* (an open mouth and repeated coughing indicating the desire to take the floor), and *postures* (agitating one's body to show the desire of taking the floor).

d) ***Affect displays*** are involuntary cues to *feelings and emotional states.* They include *facial movements* such as *smiles, frowns,* and *sneers* (indicating anger, disgust, fear, happiness, sadness, and surprise), and *postures* (a face-to-face position indicating openness, a back turning position indicating refusal).

e) ***Adaptors*** involve *release of physical tension.* They may be either the means for tension release or the results of tension release: scratching your head may be an instrumental behaviour to relieve an itch; moment-to-moment wiggles and jiggles of various body parts, biting your nails, or clicking your pen may result merely from random nervous system activity.

A very important aspect of **kinesics** (the *study of body movement*) is the distinction between *innate* and *acquired gestures*. I. Eibl-Eibesfeldt (Descamps, 1989, 174) argued that part of the gestures common to both men and animals are ***universal gestures***: *meeting and greeting* are done by raising one's head and uplifting one's eyes (and smiling), *menacing* by raising one's shoulders (and showing one's teeth), *submitting* by bowing one's head and dropping one's eyes.

Knowing the ***cultural determination of gestures*** is of greatest importance for people involved in business. Thus, D. Efron (Descamps, 1989, 177) showed that *Jews* have moderate, irregular and complex gestures and *Italians* have ample gestures, while the gestures of the 2nd immigrant generation of *Jews* and *Italians* hybridise with those of the Anglo-Saxons. L. Wylie (Descamps, 1989, 176) showed that the way people walk in the street also differs from one culture to another: *Americans* fling about their arms and move their shoulders while walking, and think that the way *Mexican-Americans* walk is servile, for they shuffle their feet and bend their backs; the *French* have a straight gait and think that Americans have a vulgar way of walking; the *Japanese* have a very rigid gait and think it is rude to turn your head after someone (that is why they turn the whole bust). Wylie also compared the different gestures for different nations and showed that: Europeans clap their hands to applaud and the Tibetans to chase the demons; Europeans hiss to disapprove and Americans to applaud; *Romanians* nod their heads to approve and the *Bulgarians* and the *Greeks* to disapprove; *Romanians* shake their heads to disapprove and the *Bulgarians* and the *Greeks* to approve.

3.2.3. Space

The use of space is a subtle but powerful factor in human social and organisational behaviour that appears to vary greatly across different cultures. In general, humans are territorial creatures who *define and defend the boundaries of their space, arrange objects in space to either suit themselves or to accomplish various purposes,* and *use space to define appropriate distance between people in interpersonal settings.*

Developing the field of **proxemics** (the *formal study of the use of space*) along the lines of Birdwhistell's kinesics, Edward Hall (Descamps, 1989, 33) identified three types of space: *fixed-feature, semi fixed-feature,* and *informal.*

a) ***Fixed-feature space*** involves stable (concrete or imaginary) boundaries that define territory. G. M. Goldhaber (Descamps, 1989, 33) pointed out that there often is a close relationship between status and territory in organisations, and identified three principles in this relationship that have the potential to influence organisational communication (to control initiating, structuring, and terminating interaction with others). Thus, the higher up you are in the organisation:

-   The more and better space you have.

-   The better protected your territory is.

-   The easier it is to invade the territory of lower-status personnel.

b) ***Semi fixed-feature space*** involves objects and fixtures (chairs, decorations, desks, equipment, files, etc.) that are somehow positioned in space, and that may or may not be intended to transmit a particular message. Thus, a high-level executive's space furnished more like a living-room than an office "communicates" an atmosphere of openness and accessibility; a lower-level manager with a cast-off military surplus desk stacked with volumes of reports and positioned as a barrier behind a door to a cramped office, the occupant's unavailability.

c) ***Informal space*** refers to the physical proximity of one person to another in interpersonal settings. E. Hall (Descamps, 1989, 34) identified four distinct informal zones in American culture:

-   *Intimate* (2.5-45 cm).

-   *Personal* (45 cm-1.20 m) (most interpersonal conversations occur in this zone).

- *Social* (1.20 m-3.6 m).

- *Public* (over 3.6 m).

Cultural determination of the space is also very important for organisational communication, no matter the type. Thus: the *Chinese* seem to require more personal distance for interaction than *Americans*, and Americans seem to require more personal distance for interaction than *Arabs* do.

3.3 Written Communication

Written communication has played an important role in human communication since times immemorial. The first written documents date from 3,200 BC, in Mesopotamia. Together with the Egyptian hieroglyphs, they were developed by other Palestinian, Syrian, etc. cultures. China also developed its own writing system, and so did Ancient Greece and Rome.

There are three types of writing: *narrative* or *syntagmatic* or *synthetic* (in which to each drawing corresponds a narrative – cave painting, Eskimo writing or Alaskan Indian writing), *morphematic* or *analytical* or *ideographic* (in which a grapheme corresponds to a sign-morpheme – Chinese writing, Egyptian writing), and *phonematic* (in which a grapheme corresponds to a phoneme (writings of all European languages) (Raţă, 2001, 113-116).

The materials on which humans wrote were diverse and they evolved in time from stone, clay, parchment, cloths, metals, papyri, etc. With the advent of print by the Gutenberg brothers, written communication changed considerably.

Surprisingly or not, the **Bible** speaks of the fact that God wrote the Ten Commandments on stone tablets (the first material used to write on), and the first printed book was the **Bible**.

With the press, written communication made a huge step ahead. Writings could be multiplied and stored in libraries, which allowed humans to communicate many things to many people; through translations, humans communicate with other cultures as well, long time after they are dead.

Written communication provides clearer expression despite the fact that there are people who master better the art of verbal communication than that of written communication. Errors in writing can be easier corrected by re-reading the written text. One can also remove from the text the phrases or paragraphs that to dot match the goal of the writing.

The era of the press was followed by the digital era. In this period, writing acquires a digital form: it can be printed on paper and also travel in time at speeds impossible to imagine a few decades ago – the speed of light.

3.4 Computer-mediated Communication (CMC)

Animal communication reaches a distance of 6 km, as is the case of the "blacksmith-frog from Brazil." (Dinu, 2000, 108) The same goes for the elephants.

Of all beings, humans alone have managed to go beyond the area of communication measurable in km, defying distance given that information travels, thanks to optic fibber, with the light speed, i.e. 299,792,458 m/s.

Virtual communication occurs in another reality, in virtual reality. Some avoid naming it "reality". In virtual reality, communication is computer mediated. The transmission channel is still mechanical, be it telegraph, telephone, fax, computer (chat, e-mail, socialisation networks, etc.).

The term *communication* has a derivative, *tele-communication* (from the Greek *tele* "far"), and a great achievement at the end of the 20th century and at the beginning of the 21st century. Many see it as an opportunity; others, such as Alain Rallet, are sceptical and worried because most (70%) of the tele-communication traffic are not only local communications – they are also communications between kinships (Cabin and Dortier, 2010, 265).

The effects are hard to anticipate since, once depending on a certain way of communicating, i.e. computer-mediated communication, you are prevented from estimating whether that way of communicating is the best or just a superficial way of spending one's time. While believing you really communicate, you risk estranging and even isolating from the real world and from all your relatives and friends. Serge Tisseron (2013, 9) said that in this new world foreign people become close people and close people become estranged people.

This possibility will be studied in the framework of empiric research characteristic of this book and one of the hypotheses of my research.

It is undoubtedly that the Internet has brought about a true *revolution*, and communication has undergone notable changes that have fathered a new branch of sociology, *Internet sociology*: we have all the reasons to believe that soon there will appear a new branch of *Internet sociology, sociology of communication in socialisation networks*. This will be absolutely necessary in a decade where, at the end of 2013, there were 1,230,000,000,000 Facebook accounts, of which 7,200,000 in Romania alone. (*Facebook: 10 years of social networking,* in numbers. Online: http://www.theguardian.com/news/datablog/2014/feb/04/facebook -in-numbers-statistics)

In January 2013, the countries with the most Facebook users were as shown in Figure 3.1 below.

Likewise, in early 2013, in regards to Facebook's mobile usage, the figures were those in Figure 3.2 below.

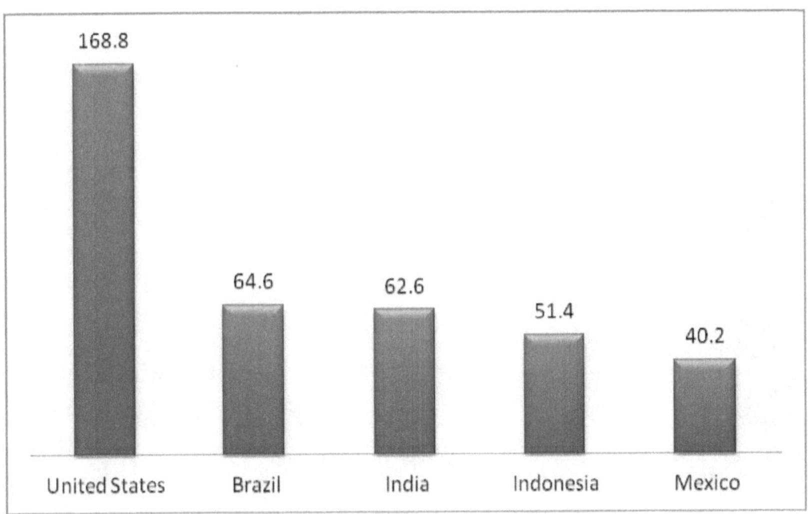

Figure 3.1 Countries with the most Facebook users in January 2013 (in millions of members)

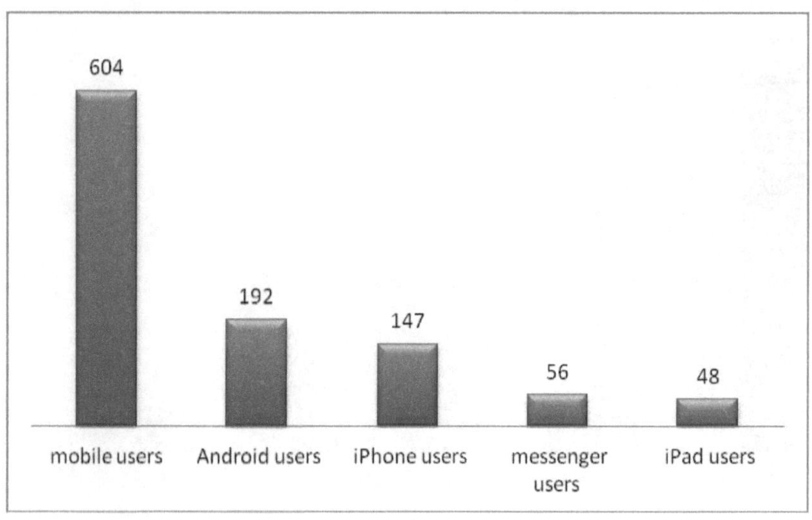

Figure 3.2 Facebook's mobile usage (in millions of users)

4. Levels of Communication

As for the number of interlocutors. Communication has several levels, starting from only two interlocutors and going to a mass of people, via smaller groups of people.

The diversity of types of communication, from this perspective, ranges between *one to one* (interpersonal communication) to *planetary* (mass communication).

4.1 Dyadic Interpersonal Communication

Te term *dyad* has been defined as two people engaged in face-to-face interaction (O'Sullivan et al., 2001, 105). Interpersonal communication can be mediated by such technologies as telephone, television, computer, etc.

This type of communication involves only two participants that communicate at leisure, without too much formalism: "the interlocutors are not hindered by anybody and, therefore, by inhibition as it sometimes happens." (Fârte, 2004, 123)

We believe that this type of communication is the most natural since the interlocutors emit their messages in turn (verbal messages) and also simultaneously (bon-verbal messages). While one of them speaks, the other one agrees or disagrees by crossing the arms, by making faces, etc., which changes the content of the message: "Both the source and the receiver are close to one another, and the feed-back is almost instantaneous." (Ştefănescu, 2009, 145)

The communication scheme is no longer the classical one (sender-receiver): the two interlocutors exchange roles and influence each other mutually: "the effects do not constitute elective presences in the scheme of communication, but indispensable elements since there is no message 'without traces' on the receiver, be they cognitive, affective, or behavioural effects." (Dinu, 2004, 40)

Depending on the responses of the interlocutor, the message can be changed and adapted to the partner of communication.

Since this type of communication is increasingly frequent in virtual communication due to the sue of technological discoveries (telephone, computer, etc.), we need to asks ourselves if there is an interpersonal relationship between the two interlocutors communicating via a monitor be it touch screen.

Joseph DeVito (1986, 72-75) identifies five conditions for efficient interpersonal communication: openness, solicitude, empathy, positive attitude and equality. From this point of view, all five conditions can be met by two communicators using an sms as a communication channel or the e-mail, or socialisation networks; what misses here, is the continuous adaptation of communication because virtual communication is an illustration of the linear model of communication of Shannon and Weaver (where the sender is only an sender and the receiver is only a receiver). Though the sequences are short, as it happens in chat, the fractures are barriers in efficient communication.

Computer-mediated communication is interpersonal communication marked by errors caused by the impossibility of using non-verbal language, by the fracture of the suites question-answer, and by the level of noise that can affect one of the interlocutors unknowingly.

Interpersonal communication leads to the development of personality. Ever since birth, a child learns from the one-to-one communication with his/her mother, then he/she learns to share his/her own opinions, to accept the opinions of the others, to negotiate and/or develop criticism. Interpersonal communication relies on inborn skills and also on competencies developed during the educational process or purely and simply acquired during interpersonal interactions. In this type of communication one develops his/her perceptive skill understood as "avoiding errors in understanding our interlocutor." (Agabrian, 2008, 41)

At the beginning of the 21ˢᵗ century, when society emphasises mass communication, individuals have the same need for personal communication (*one-to-one*, *face-to-face*); because they do not have much time or the availability to move, they prefer mediated communication to meet his/her need for interpersonal relationships.

4.2 Group Communication

Group communication is another form of interpersonal communication; what differs is the number of people involved. We use the term group in its retrained meaning – 3 to 30 people. Ethnic groups do not count here since they can number millions of individuals.

The form of communication usually studied in sociology is not interpersonal (dyadic), but the one involving a community, i.e. a group, an audience or a mass of people. We try to define all these forms below from the perspective of virtual communication, the main topic of this book.

A group is represented by two or more people that interact in such a way that each of them influenced the other people and is, in his/her turn influenced by the other people (Forsyth, 1983, 8).

Everybody belongs to one or more groups: family, class, club, friends who share common interests, etc.

Communication involves space and time closure, common interests and/or experiences, interaction with other members of the group, time for relationships to consolidate, etc.

Communication acts within the group are not spontaneous; they are intentional and have a precise goal, one or several common objectives that need this organisational structure. Within a group, communication is better if there is a leader that guides communication acts and establishes the limits of interaction between group members.

Group communication is increasingly frequent in the virtual sphere, both through e-mail (where there is the possibility of developing groups) and particularly through socialisation networks (where they develop networks and groups based on common interests).

4.3 Public Communication

Public communication is the type of communication that goes beyond groups organised depending on different criteria and that aims at changing peers' behaviour.

Public communication is about "involving people in activities and behaviours that suppose individual wellbeing and collective welfare." (Ştefănescu, 2010, 241) We all speak of "collective welfare" but we should bear in mind that this "welfare" is subjective.

Public communication belongs with public administration, non-governmental organisations – therefore, we will not insist on this type of communication.

We will try to analyse this topic from the perspective of an individual who communicates virtually using a Facebook account or any other socialisation network and who, by posting on the wall, communicates publicly.

Some authors question the legitimacy of trying to change the behaviour of our peers for the sake of collective welfare.

The two main means of public communication are persuasion and constraint, with "the latter intervening only when the former failed." (Tran and Stănciugelu, 2003, 140) But isn't this another form of manipulation? We will not tackle persuasion or constraint because they belong rather to the spheres of politics, institutions, publicity, etc. than to the virtual sphere.

But there is still the moral aspect of the fact that sometimes the private area of an individual (even the most intimate one) is made public, which becomes embarrassing for a common sense person:

> "Twenty-five years ago, under the rule of Ceauşescu's Securitate, the Romanians would protect their privacy fiercely. Nowadays, in the time of Internet socialisation, we display our personal life in front of everybody... Facebook has changed, before everything else, the way in which we perceive privacy and introduced, globally, the display of one's own life on the Internet." (Voinea, Delcea and Varninschi, *Efectele Facebook. Cum am ajuns să ne spionăm între noi şi ce spune SRI despre monitorizarea reţelelor sociale*. Online: http://adevarul.ro/tech/retele-sociale/video-efectele-facebook-ajuns-spionam-spune-sri-despre-monitorizarea-retelelor-sociale1_53971dd80d133766a875783a/index.html.).

Maybe the most comprehensive theoretical framework for personal information-related behaviours in the online environment is that of Beldad, de Jong and Steehouder (2011), who examine the impact of trust and inducements on Internet users' willingness to share personal information and synthesise the most important postulates from theories in communication, social psychology and sociology.

Peggy Noonan, author of Ronald Reagan's speeches while President of the USA, wrote, for *Wall Street Journal*, an article titled *Making the angels blush, or This is not how to treat a lady*, where she protests against the invasion of the public space by advertisings to contraceptive products, to female hygiene products. She says that she experiences the same feelings when politicians are asked very private questions about their families and are pressed to state their position about sex-related topics just because somebody somewhere decided that it should be the political topic number one, the breaking news topic (Dobson, 2012, 79).

Now, that everybody can express freely using mainly media channels, the demarcation line between private and public communication is increasingly thinner: the private invades, even violates the public sphere, turning it into a place where not only angels, but also common sense people start blushing – even those in front of monitors who benefit from technological discoveries (telephone, radio, television, computer linked to the Internet) to force the limits of public communication and take it to a level that lacks politeness and respect for human dignity.

Gheorghe-Ilie Fârte (2004, 127-128) identifies six remarkable constancies of public communication:

- Its context is formal;

- The sender dominates with authority the situation of communication;

- The receiver is busy with a relatively numerous and sometimes heterogeneous audience;

- When the channel has no technical components to make the message pass, the signals emitted by the locators tend to turn more obvious than in normal situations (at the theatre, the across speak very loudly and make obvious gestures to communicate with people in the audience far from the stage);

- The obstacles to communication are relatively numerous (noises, visual obstacles, etc.);

-   The retroaction of communication is poor, i.e. limited to certain non-verbal behaviours.

In mediated public communication, there are no formal constraints: courts, churches, schools, parliaments, universities and conference halls are areas that mark communication in a concrete way. In the virtual environment, all these constraints are annulled and we believe this is the reason why there are side-slipping and confusion in public communication.

4.4 Mass Communication

In the last 100 years of mass communication has represented not only a new dimension of the process of communication but covers an increasingly larger place. Mass communication is a form of mediated communication in which an organisation sues technology as a medium to communicate with a wider audience (Baran and Davis, 2000, 9).

We believe that McQuail's definition of mass communication is equally important, but less detailed: a new dimension of the social process of communication, the result of the invention of new means of multiplying and disseminating messages – print, photography, wireless telegraph, etc., and of the development of new social institutions based on the use of these techniques (McQuail, 1999, 172).

Another definition that we consider more complex sees mass communication as any form of communication in which messages – public messages that use a medium to be disseminated – address a wide audience in an indirect (because the communication partners are distanced in time and space) and unilateral (which excludes role exchange between emitter and receiver) way (Van Cuilenburg, Scholten and Noomen, 1998, 41).

From the point of view of the specificity of mass communication, it has four features: "institutionalised character of the sender; socialising, collective and multiple character of communication; indirect, mediated and impersonal character of communication; unidirectional character of communication, lack or small size of feedback." (Ştefănescu, 2009, 185)

Mass communication incorporates newspapers (including online versions), radio, television, book, music, etc.

This type of communication is not the topic of this book, but its study is useful because virtual communication is intensely promoted by mass communication; it is not a coincidence, therefore, that most computer users also have socialisation network accounts. Figure 4.1 below shows a list of virtual communities with more than 100 million active users.

Moreover, another similarity between mass communication and virtual communication is that they are both technologically mediated (by a computer and by the Internet).

Mass communication is the domain of professionals, particularly media trusts, and this raises an issue that we should take into account: the risk of manipulation. I believe it was excessively sincere to admit, in an ad of the 1990s, that "Publicity does not harm anyone, it manipulates." (Slama-Cazacu, 2000, 52)

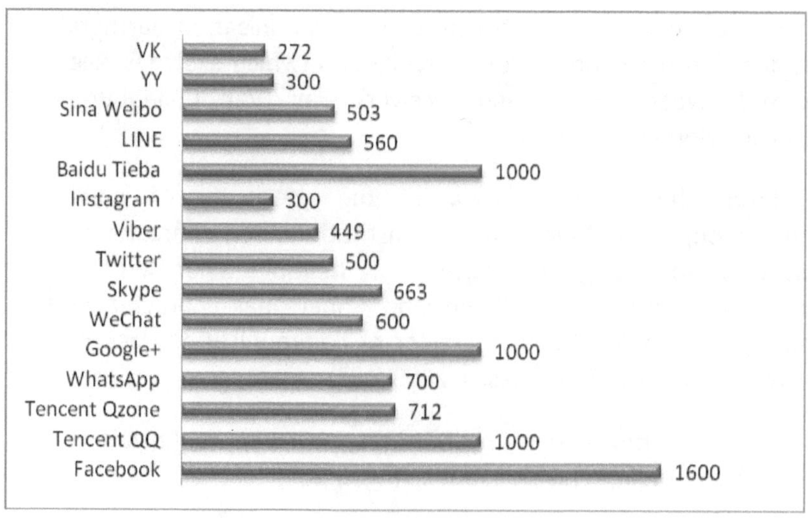

Source:http://en.wikipedia.org/wiki/List_of_virtual_communities_with_more_than_100_million_active_users

Figure 4.1 Virtual communities with more than 100 million active users (in millions of users)

From the way in which a producer designs his show to the way in which an editor chooses the news and presents them, and particularly in the case of the ads, there is a tendency to manipulate; unfortunately, media consumers cannot always resist manipulation. For instance, images and frames in ads are carefully displayed and some of them are presented so shortly that they are not perceived in the conscious register but are interpreted by the brain and reach the sub-conscient.

Emil Bartoş (in Neagoe, 2011, 208) noted that "the industrial revolution brought about a new type of entertainment: the show business. Telephone, photography, radio, movie, television and, finally, the Internet, have been exploited at a maximum. The power of influence of mass communication moved to the field of image. Once, events were told or read, which allowed the listener to practice his/her imagination. The appearance of moving images turned the listener into a spectator. The new type of participant participates, in fact, very little."

Media specialists are only professionals in different branches of science and the manipulation danger is high. The effects of mediated communication are undoubtedly very high and intentional, as obvious in the case of ads. If the effect were not high, they would not invest huge amounts in publicity, particularly in television and, more recently, on the Internet. They talk about "publicity-persuasive campaigns." (Drăgan, 2007, 258) These persuasive methods need a complex effort and the four techniques used are images, humour, sex, and replication (Werner and Tankard, 2004, 201).

What is, in fact, manipulation? It designates the action of determining a social actor (person, group, community) to think and act in a way compatible with the interests of the initiator and not with his/her own interests, an initiator who distorts the truth purposely creating the impression of freedom of thought and decision. (Zamfir and Vlăsceanu, 1998, 332)

The owners of socialisation networks have found a very intelligent way to manipulate over 2,000,000,000 people who have a total of 5,700,000,000 accounts (Cojocaru, *Adobe a publicat lista celor mai mari rețele de socializare pe Internet*. Online: http://incomemagazine.ro/articole/adobe-a-publicat-lista-celor-mai-mari-retele-de-socializare-pe-internet), many of which check their accounts to see what is new, to play games, to look at something and to give likes.

There, they see ads for goods and services that they do not want but that have a great influence on their brains, on their desires, etc. In addition, they are monitored to see what their interests are (depending on the sites they access) and they are supplied with offers by companies that pay the access to the user's brains. Recently, they have discovered that even written words not published on Facebook account are stored, which points to some kind of though control.

In regional Internet markets, Facebook penetration is, per continents and parts of continents, as shown in Figure 4.2 below:

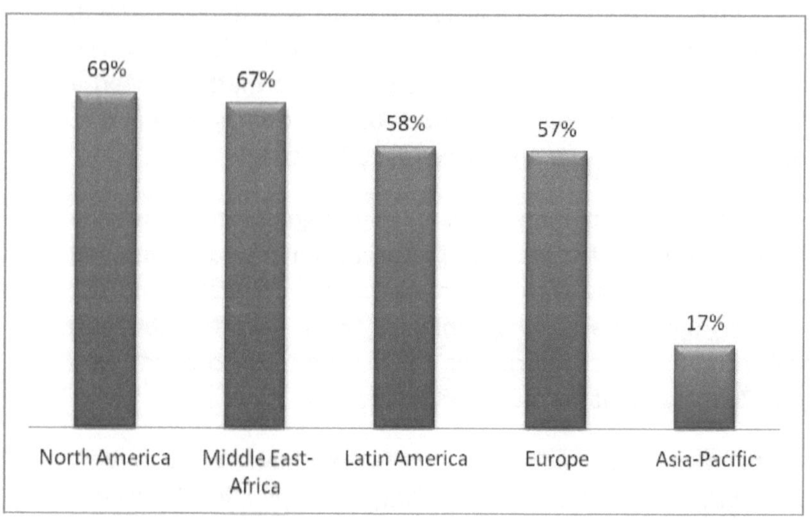

Figure 4.2 Facebook penetration in regional Internet markets

Communication is increasingly persuasive and manipulative, a thing Ion Drăgan anticipated back in 1980 when he spoke of "an informative, influencing activity aiming at shaping and changing ideas, attitudes and behaviours." (Drăgan, 1980, 310)

Facebook manipulation takes place through the entry gate of information to the brains, human eye. Jesus, in His Sermon on the Mount, said, "The eye is the lamp of the body. If your eyes are healthy, your whole body will be full of light." (Matthew 6:22)

It is interesting to note that virtual communication, particularly in socialisation networks, uses the same persuasive techniques.

Since images tell more than words, we present below the world map of the most popular social networking sites by country (Figure 4.3):

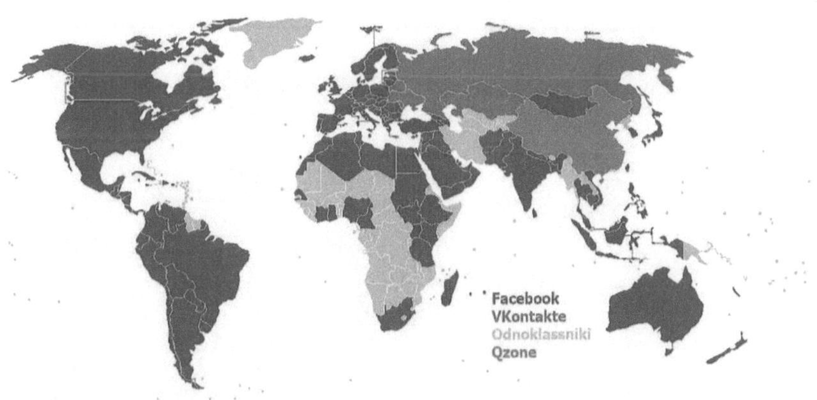

Source:http://en.wikipedia.org/wiki/Facebook#mediaviewer/ File:Social_networks.jpg

Figure 4.3 The most popular social networking sites by country

The question is whether it is moral to use persuasive techniques to reach expected effects if they do not serve the interests of the individual?! Do we have any chance in the fight started by the mass media not necessarily against us?! But surely in its own interests and in the interest of its clients. We can keep our values, beliefs, principles in front of this roller that tends to turn us into a mass of individuals incapable of thinking (Van Cuilenburg, Scholten and Noomen, 1998, 40).

5. Barriers to Communication

Communication is neither good, nor bad: it depends on the character of the communicator, on the perspicacity of the receiver, on the noise level, etc. But there are obstacles or barriers that prevent communication from reaching its goal, i.e. "effective exchange of ideas or thoughts" (*Barriers to Communication*. Online: http://www.businessdictionary.com/definition/barriers-to-communication.html). According to the same source, such barriers include *social differences*, *gender differences*, *cultural differences*, *prejudices* and the *organisational environment*.

Stancu Şerb (2007) identifies four types of obstacles in public relations that we present below from the perspective of the relationships in computer mediated communication and particularly in socialisation networks.

These barriers to communication are tackled below aiming at comparing face-to-face communication (specific to public relations) and virtual communication. What we want to see is if barriers to communication can also be considered barriers to virtual communication.

5.1 Social Barriers

"Are considered social barriers: professional environments, extraprofessional frameworks, traditions and customs, age and gender, social models, and appurtenance to a cult or religious sect." (Şerb, 2007, 50)

These barriers are easier to overrun when communication is mediated because, hidden by a monitor, everybody pretends he/she is what he/she wants to be. There are more and more cases in which different communicators pretend to have certain professions, ages, cars, etc.; with no more barriers in communication, these communicators can easily communicate with people with other interests and orientations.

5.2 Cultural Barriers

This type of barriers refers to "language, vocabulary, social level, intellectual level, as well as to some motivations that are determined by one's personal interest in the topic." (Şerb, 2007, 51)

It seems that there are no longer, in virtual communication, such barriers: there are, online, programmes that translate, pre-established texts for conversation (how to initiate and close a conversation) – in virtually every spoken language. We receive all kind of communications from unknown people who offer certain things, make proposals, etc. Only Google Translator makes us see it like a kind of barrier because it does not translate acceptably, but this will be solved in the near future.

Vulgar, indecent phrases can be replaced with aphorisms found on the Internet that are meant to impress the interlocutor who, in most cases, does not have the necessary culture to identify a quotation from Einstein or Pascal.

5.3 Psychological Barriers

There are several psychological barriers that hinder communication. Among them, Stancu Şerb (2007, 55) enumerates emotivity, aggressiveness, timidity and affectivity. They are very difficult to perceive in virtual communication.

Emotivity visible in changes of the face traits, changes of respiration, changes of the voice, etc., which a keyboard cannot transmit; therefore, communication is not only poorer, but it also fails to supply important information on a virtual interlocutor.

Aggressiveness is a natural trend unwanted in humans. The solution is to master oneself and not to hide it. We do not like aggressive people, but can we feel the aggressiveness of a person with whom we communicate virtually? Can we know how often he/she beats the table with his/her fist or breaks a glass by throwing it to the wall?

Timidity is a type of defensive, anxious and hesitating behaviour. It is certainly seen rather as a defect than as a quality. It is now certain that many of the bold ones on the Facebook are, in fact, shy: in real life, they do not dare look somebody in the eye or utter vulgar words. Overcoming shyness supposes a process of continuous development of self-confidence and of trust in the others, of committing about major issues. Treating shyness through boldness in virtual communication leads to a kind of schizophrenia difficult to treat even by specialists.

Affectivity is a type of sensitivity that can lead to a weakening of the capacity of acting of social actors. Affectivity is a quality that makes us all pleasant, but it can also be a defect because affective communication mediated by technical means weakens the capacity of action of the people involved. They cannot say "yes" with a firm tone and, moreover, they cannot say "no" when this is the only answer possible.

Alman, Valenzi and Hodgetts (1985, 528-531) also note a few psychological barriers to efficient communication: emotional blockage, different communication registers of communication actors, sender's inability to speak up properly, and personal differences of the communicators in relation to the others.

5.4 Physical Barriers

These barriers consist in physical appearance, look, tics, fatigue, etc. All these physical barriers to communication are no longer perceived in virtual communication because "the virtual" is the prolongation of "the real", of an entity that can have very similar or even identical features with those of a corresponding real object. In the virtual environment, physical appearance, tics, or fatigue become unimportant and difficult to perceive thus ceasing to be barriers to communication.

If we look at these limitations of social, cultural, physiological, and physical nature, they almost no longer are barriers in virtual communication. It seems advantageous to race in a horse race without obstacles; in fact, without these barriers, communication is no longer restrained in a computer-mediated environment; however, people need more than that and it is at that point that someone who is a good communicator in the virtual sphere are quite different in the real sphere.

Virtual communication is confronted with these social barriers and, though it seems much easier to overcome these obstacles, virtual communicators are exposed to risks: thus, what seems to be very good in the beginning, can turn later on into a huge problem.

6. Communication and Human Relationships

Communication is one of the most important components of human relationships. Argyle and Henderson (1985, 25) carried out a trans-cultural study on three continents (Europe, Asia and Africa) regarding human inter-relational rules in different cultures and discovered four trans-cultural rules that could be considered universal:

-   The need to observe somebody else's privacy, loneliness and secrets;

-   The necessity to look the interlocutor in the eye while talking to him/her;

-   The interdiction of talking with anybody else something confidential;

-   The interdiction of criticising somebody publicly.

We need socialisation, communication, belonging to a community, family, affection, and God!

Commenting Abraham Maslow's model, Zamfir and Vlăsceanu (1982, 77) noted, "Man fundamentally needs to love and be loved; he needs strong affective relationships that support him psychologically. In other words, he needs family, love, friends, children, etc."

6.1 Relationship with the Divinity

The highest form of interpersonal communication is between man and his Creator. God is a being that reveals Himself, who invested in humankind and who continued and continues to communicate with His creation. The ability of communicating with God is one of the things that differentiate us from the rest of God's creation (Tripp, 2013, 13).

The means of communication between man and God are very different because God made us able to communicate with Him. People do not communicate with God not because they do not have this skill, but for reasons related to their availability and human sensitivity of distinguishing God's voice. The fact that we do not really hear God's voice does not mean that He does not speak at all. It is rather common, even in our strictly human relationships, to not hear the ones who talk to us (Willard, 1990, 75).

We take into account this kind of *man – God* relationship because, in a way, it is similar to virtual communication: it supposes a certain distance between man and God, it is often mediated (by angels, prophets, etc.); and it is coded (therefore, the receiver needs to be able to decode it).

God's clearest, safest and most common way of communicating is through the Holy Scriptures. In this case, God is the transmitter and man is the receiver. Though the **Bible** was written thousands of years ago, it has a fantastic relevance for people living at two millennia distance from the moment it was written. In fact, God's words are principles applicable to concrete situations. The most frequent way in which man (the transmitter) communicates with God (the receiver) is the prayer. A prayer is about verbal language, non-verbal language, and emotional communication.

Besides these two forms of common communication, there are extraordinary means through which God communicates with men. Below are some of these means:

- *Communication through angels*. American scientist Mortimer Adler (1982) speaks of how other scientists opposed his idea of including angels among the greatest ideas of Western minds (Adler, 1982). Angel means "emissary" or "messenger". Angels are supernatural beings used by God to carry certain messages to humans. We admit that communication through angels is not the most frequent type of communication between God and men, but it is a type of communication found in the **Bible** and in the experiences of different people who have a close relationship with their Creator.

- *Communication through prophets*. Unlike angels, prophets are human messengers who receive certain general or particular messages from God and then share these messages with nations or other people. Prophets bring God's message and announce things God will do in the future. "Who then is like me? Let him proclaim it. Let him declare and lay out before me what has happened since I established my ancient people, and what is yet to come – yes, let them foretell what will come." (Isaiah 44:7) The simplest way to check a prophecy is its achievement. A prophet has to say the truth, and the materialisation of his words is the proof of the truthfulness of his message.

- *Communication through visions and dreams*. The two resemble very much since they both involve images and words; the only difference is that, in visions, the receiver is awake, while in a dream, he is asleep. A dream asks for a stronger, sometimes more difficult interpretation effort of a kind that a vision does not require (Willard, 1990, 107).

Only those who communicate with God on a daily basis – through the reading of the Holy Scriptures and through prayer – acquire the art of conversation with the Creator and enjoy these extraordinary communication experiences; though not imperatively necessary, they are possible and enrich virtual communication with God beyond simple words.

Communication with God, like communication with people, changes even human physiognomy. Sad news, critiques, encouragements have immediate effects on a man's face. "The LORD would speak to Moses face to face, as one speaks to a friend. Then Moses would return to the camp, but his young aide Joshua son of Nun did not leave the tent." (Exodus 33:11) As a result, "they saw that his face was radiant. Then Moses would put the veil back over his face until he went in to speak with the LORD." (Exodus 34:35)

6.2 Relationship with Friends

Friendship is one of the oldest and most beautiful ways of interacting between people (no matter their age) and between people and God. Language dictionaries define the word friend as follows: "1. a person attached to another by feelings of affection or personal regard. 2. a person who gives assistance; patron; supporter: *friends of the Boston Symphony.* 3. a person who is on good terms with another; a person who is not hostile: *Who goes there? Friend or foe?* 4. a member of the same nation, party, etc. 5. (initial capital letter) a member of the Religious Society of Friends; a Quaker. 6. a person associated with another as a contact on a social-networking website: *We've never met, but we're Facebook friends."* (*The American Heritage Dictionary of the English Language.* Online: http://www.yourdictionary.com/virtual#americanheritage) Affection is the invisible link providing emotional support within a relationship.

Friendship has "different degrees of intimacy – from simple 'acquaintances' to 'intimate' friend. We usually have several 'acquaintances', few 'close friends' and fewer 'intimate friends.'" (Răşcanu, 2007, 99)

There are numerous books on friendship – both fiction and literature (psychology), but the Book of the Books in Christianity is the **Bible** – and it speaks a lot about friendship. Thus, Eliphaz from Teman, Job's friend, urges the latter, while experiencing suffering, "Submit to God and be at peace with him; in this way prosperity will come to you." (Job 22:21) The holy text says not only that friendship with God is possible and desirable: it also tells the benefits of friendship with God for man, i.e. *peace* (with himself, with his peers and with God) and *happiness* (so much desired and searched for since times immemorial).

As for inter-human friendship, the **Bible** supplies some extraordinary examples:

- The friendship between David and Jonathan. Though Saul, Jonathan's father, hated David because the latter was more popular and appreciated than himself, he manages to overcome all the obstacles and proves to be a true friend;

- The friendship between Jesus and his disciples: "I tell you, my friends, do not be afraid of those who kill the body and after that can do no more." (Luke 12:4) and "The Son of Man came eating and drinking, and you say, 'Here is a glutton and a drunkard, a friend of tax collectors and sinners." (Luke 7:34). This kind of friendship with people disapproved by the society was not profitable at all, but it was seen as an investment of God's Son in people not for what they represented but what for what they might become.

According to the saying "Dog is man's best friend", this relationship of friendship has also reached the *man – animal* level. In our world, this relationship of friendship hides a serious problem – failure in human relationships, which leads, in time, to isolation and refuge in a relationship with a pet.

We believe that man has been increasingly busy, socially distanced and more selfish since the end of the 20th century, which made him fail nurturing significant friendship relationships. This is the reason why virtual relationships got to be so important for people with tens of virtual friends but no real friends.

During our counselling sessions, we meet an increasing number of young people who confess they have no true friend. Asked about virtual friends (as used on Facebook), they acknowledge having hundreds, maybe even thousands of friends: unfortunately, they do not go to parties together, do not have significant conversations together, do not walk together, do not dine together, do not practice sports together, do not go to church together, and do not live together in a community.

"The erotic-sentimental attraction shares a lot in pre-teenage and particularly teenage." (Mitrofan, 1984, 165) Thus, though they are very active on socialisation networks or on "second life" sites trying to fill the void of communication with virtual communication, they become increasingly sadder, more lonely, less confident, more hostile and, unfortunately, more depressed.

Significant friendship relationships influence man's health state and well-being, reduce stress, provide social support and reduce stressors.

We have been created with certain needs that are either fulfilled or they do not operate at optimum level. Virtual friendship is acknowledged as a form of inter-human relationship but it is not fully satisfactory because man needs verbal, non-verbal, and paraverbal communication, touch, etc. to meet Maslow's 3rd rank needs (family, affection, relationships, affiliation).

6.3 Relationships within the Couple

Communication is determining in couple relationships: here, we refer mainly to marriage and concubinage – an increasingly frequent phenomenon in both Europe and the U.S.A.

What gathers together two people in a couple relationship is love – an extremely complex thing that brings together two people with their intimate structure and expectations.

Besides physical attraction – that seems to play an overrated role in society – there needs to be sincere communication and a type of relationship between the two partners, relationship impossible without intense communication.

For a couple to resist in time, communication needs to be permanent. All the statistics made in the last years in Europe and the U.S.A. show that divorce and separation rate is increasing because of the lack of commitment, emotional support, or privacy. Excellent marriages start with excellent communication. Unhappy marriages root in miscommunication (Rich and Kravitz, 2006, 49).

There is communication at the beginning of a relationship and communication makes things evolve. There are, on the Internet, numbers of matchmaking sites where everybody can meet everybody and fall in love. Though these people are already involved in a relationship, there is a great risk of emotional attachment to an unknown person. In addition, people who fall in love tend to see things in rose. (Hendrick and Hendrick, 1988, 178) Virtual communication leads in many cases to falling in love without even having met the other: the feeling is for somebody one has seen only in a few photos (some of which are edited) and with whom he/she has changes a few more or less original lines. In a super-sexualised world, it is easy to understand why teenagers get to have intercourse at very young ages. Virtual communication burns important stages in a couple's life because it jumps directly to sex.

I interviewed a woman who had been sequestrated and threatened for months after communicating with a man who claimed to be a good respectable person but who proved to be a convicted offender.

Mrs K. Was married and she has a child. She has a good material life but, because of some problems with her husband, she divorced. She kept their child (aged 12). From curiosity and wishing to meet somebody who understand, support and love her, she opened a personal account on a matrimonial site to communicate with different males and meet her affective needs. The "opportunity" came relatively quickly: she met a man of her age who seemed respectable and who pretended to be a secret service officer. They started an intense virtual communication. The man seemed to be the right person for her and her son. They communicated for three months and then she decided to invite him to her place. Then the ordeal started: she was sequestrated, extorted, threatened, abused, filmed in different sexual hypostases, etc. It was only six months later that she escaped from the hands of the "respectable sir." At the trial, the judge asked her who had invited the man to her place and she admitted she had. Then the judge asked how long did it take them to have sex and the answer was "five minutes." The conclusion was: *there had been no rape and no sequestration because she had invited the man to her place and had consensual sex.*

We have selected the details above because they show that, in virtual communication, knowledge is extremely superficial and the easy passage from admiration to attachment and then to love can have serious sentimental and physical effects on people. Acquaintances on the Internet are marvellous and captivating because they make you feel like in a virtual novel that later turns into reality (Vaghin and Gluschai, 2006, 29). The same authors supply several case studies of which we present the following:

"I met her on a lovers' chat. Our chatting was not chatting, but continuous insulting. I had a friend at the time with which I used to chat. Suddenly, during such a chat, I was approached by a stranger. First, she behaved very strangely, very rudely, which I did not like and my virtual friend said:
-    Maybe it's a boy, not a girl!
-    Yes, maybe, I said.
What do you think I did? I decided, like an idiot, to shame on the chat the beautiful stranger! I said, "Folks, this is a man!" Yes, I acted as a coward. The next day I found out it was a girl, which made me happy. I started to talk to her more and more, to ask her how she looked like, what she did for a living and all those stupid standard questions. I said everything I had to say. Of course, I got impatient and I asked her to show me a photo of her. In the photo, I saw a girl unique from all points of view, a wonderful stranger. I fell in love. It was love at first sight. From outside, all this seems bizarre, unreal. Unreal indeed because she lived in another town, in another country, and this made me sad. But then we agreed to meet and suddenly I felt relieved. This is how I fell in love virtually. But nothing seemed unusual to me, I was already in love. Deep in my soul, everything was real. No barrier frightened me. My beautiful stranger also loved me! Everything was purely and simply wonderful! We were hidden on the chat, in a private area; we took a certain distance and did not show up. Everybody knew we were lovers. Everything came from our singing and dancing souls! But love is not eternal: everything collapsed, our love melted out until it stopped... You might ask, 'How did it all happen?' It simply did. Because of an old acquaintance. He decided to tell me all kind of innuendos and this offended me (I omitted to tell you that my beloved was married). As for the innuendos and lies of my friend, they were not private: everybody could read them. Nothing could have happened unless her husband saw them. Yes, her legitimate husband! She was not on the chat, but he did! In short, he

copied our opinions on the beautiful stranger and showed them the next day to his wife. This is how our love died. I tried very hard to show her that it was not the truth and that it was all an error, but in vain. She disappeared from the Internet. But I do love her! This is virtual love!" (Vaghin and Gluschai, 2006, 30-32)

Virtual communication relationships have consequences on real life. It is easy to imagine what could have happened if the two strangers – from different countries and at least one of them married – had met.

We would like to advance the concept of *premature intimacy* starting from these two case studies. Intimate relationships should develop little by little, through real knowledge, through dates, time spent together, touches, gestures, etc., turning into "a close, familiar, and usually affectionate or loving personal relationship with another person or group." (*Dictionary.com Unabridged.* Online: http://dictionary.reference.com/browse/intimacy) Virtual communication does not provide all this: communication is superficial despite the fact that the subjects might find it deep: intimacy is premature, it burns some important stages and brought to sexual relationships, i.e. to immoral relationships in unmarried people and adultery in married people.

Communication is absolutely necessary as both a prelude and an additive in couple relationships; virtual communication cannot bear alone the burden of this responsibility. If this type of communication leads to a date, the subjects think they have a high level of intimacy: in fact, intense virtual communication makes two complete strangers feel emotionally close.

A variety of psychological interpretations of the concept of intimacy in terms of its motivations, characteristics and functions is supplied by Bruce Barton (2008).

6.4 Parent-Child Relationship

Communication between parents and children is a must in the development of the latter. "Relationships between parents and children suppose a particular socially filtered mechanism based on communication as a model, a conduct pattern." (Răşcanu, 2007, 112)

This type of communication differs depending on the child's age – non-verbal communication with infants, answers to elementary, primary and secondary school child's questions, teenage (when parents need to accept the shift of communication from family to friends). Communication in family can turn very tensed sometimes engendering the so-called "generation gap." This is the time when a parent realises how difficult and demanding the job of being a parent is. Interrupting communication at teenage can make teenagers feel rejected and this affects seriously the way they communicate (they can become aggressive, delinquent or even schizophrenic). The solution is avoiding conflictual communication or killing conflictual communication at a very early stage; however, the problem is that "none of those involved is willing 'to lose the fight', 'to be humiliated', 'to be considered weaker'." (Neagoe, 2007, 138)

This is a period "characterised by critical integration of sexual, cognitive, abstract maturation. Teenagers become autonomous, they develop their own system of values – it is now that they choose their future job. Parents lose their power little by little, and teenagers feel they have enough energy to define their identity." (Muntean, 2006, 236)

From a communicational point of view, "teenagers become 'experts' in not transmitting anything: they 'talk', but they do not communicate." (Rășcanu, 2007, 114)

Talking without communicating is an interesting concept: it characterises tempestuous talks on chats, on socialisation networks, on matrimonial sites where people talk or write without communicating.

Young people remove their accounts from the Facebook because they feel their parents spy on them; this is only part of the truth, because some young people communicate only virtually thus forcing their parents also to communicate virtually because this is the only way they can make their messages reach their children.

6.5 Professional Communication

Profession plays an important role in both men and women particularly in Western societies. Professional communication is extremely important because it takes most of our time. Professional communication is somehow different from other types of communication. In this case, the emphasis is no longer on affective aspects, but on practicality and money. People come to work to make money. Therefore, they need to cooperate and work in teams. There are several forms of professional relationships: boss – subordinate, colleague – colleague, teacher – pupil, etc.

Communication differs in these sub-groups of professional relationships, but on the whole some acceptable limits need to be observed from the perspective of satisfaction level and of conflict-solving.

To be efficient, these professional relationships need to overcome two major obstacles: avoiding sentimental relationships and time loss doing other things than mentioned in one's job description).

Though most conduct codes at office developed by the great multinational companies forbid sentimental relationships between colleagues, in reality this occurs frequently. Time spent together at the work place, team-building, the weakening of family relationships, disappointments, unrealistic expectations in family, the lack of affectivity during childhood, etc. can lead in many cases to unjustified emphasis on affection detrimental to money-making.

Professional communication needs to limit to the field of work; involving romance, love disillusion, marital issues not only make people waste precious time for the company, they shift to a vulnerable area where people focus on other issues that those belonging to their job description; as a result, conflicts occur between co-workers dynamiting the climate specific to progress.

The virtual component makes sentimental involvement easier because meeting a colleagues on a socialisation network not only supplies one with important information from almost all fields of life, including private ones, allowing one to flirt without being seen, to make advances to somebody to check his/her availability thus getting ready for later physical approach.

This is mainly about values and consequence: values and beliefs represent you and are obvious in all aspects of your behaviour at workplace. If you try to make your colleagues and superiors you are somebody else, you are different from what they believe you are, your true beliefs betray you (Hartley, 2005, 110).

We should not forget why we go to work – to make profit and reach welfare – and that this could help Romania overcome its economic problems whose roots have a strong ethical, moral and spiritual nature. Women and men differ as far as work satisfaction is concerned. Women are more concerned about the social aspect of their professional relationship: maybe this is why work satisfaction is, usually, higher than that of men. Satisfaction needs to come from work, from well-done things, from financial reward because a workplace does not provide sentimental or sexual satisfaction.

Another issue that we are taking into account is that of avoiding time loss because of other fields than that of one's workplace. Most often, people working in an office do not use time with high efficiency. Many employees play computer games during their office time, or access different sites (not related to their work), or they purely and simply post, comment, read, etc. on socialisation networks. Though contrary to the job ethics, these practices are frequent because people feel like "killing the time" this way or smoking or drinking coffee.

Communication is very important in professional relationships, but it needs to be kept within the limits of one's workplace and of the strict nature of this type of relationship.

7. Risks of Communication

Though there are so many benefits of communication that we can see in our everyday life – since morning, when we kiss our wives and kids, till evening, when we read a text from the **Bible** and pray (direct communication with God), at our work place where we communicate with our colleagues, upon dinner with a business partner, when we correct our children's homework, when we scold our children for what they did not do properly or encourage them for what they did well. There are, however, in all this, communication risks and challenges that we should not deny or neglect.

7.1 Communication and Lie

Communication needs to be true. Unfortunately, many acts of communication have to do more with lies ("1. a false statement made with deliberate intent to deceive; an intentional untruth; a falsehood. 2. something intended or serving to convey a false impression; imposture: *His flashy car was a lie that deceived no one."* – *Dictionary.com Unabridged.* Online: http://dictionary.reference.com/browse/lie) than with truths (1. the <u>true</u> or actual state of a matter: *He tried to find out the truth.* 2. conformity with fact or reality; verity: *the truth of a statement.* – *Dictionary.com Unabridged.* Online: http://dictionary.reference.com/browse/truth). "No matter how uncomfortable it might seem, [lie] exists and we need to take it into account." (Albu, 2008, 217)

Truth is one, lies are several. Believing in all communication acts is infantile and naive. People are not always sincere in interpersonal relationships: newspaper news is sometimes disinformation, and we have often been deceived by colleagues, journalists, politicians, etc.

In the current context, lie "begins to make sense, to belong to social conventions thus losing its malignant character." (Chiru, 2009, 96) We believe that this adaptation to the environment leads to a relativisation of the truth, dangerous since it engenders suspicion and leads to mistrust which, in its turn, leads to unhealthy communication. Lies not only distort facts, they also destroy people's self-confidence − a self-confidence they need so much to communicate between them (Tripp, 2013, 33).

According to a study carried out in 1975 (Chiru, 2009, 168), 62% of conversations are deceiving acts; 30% are lies, 5% are exaggerations, 29% are half-truths, 3% are secrets, 32% are diversions and 1% are truths (Figure 7.1).

Authors such as Ognev and Russev (2005, 7) detail lack of truth in fabrication, deceit and lie.

Though truth should belong with all communications, this is not always the case and it does not help interpersonal relationships. Some kind of prudence should guide us and protect us from those who no longer can distinguish truth from lie because their consciousness is asleep.

After evaluating several studies carried out in the last decades, Irena Chiru drew the conclusion that lie can be detected based on some "non-verbal indices relevant for truth/untruth." (Chiru, 2009, 172) Thus, when lying, there is agitation and hesitation manifest in binding one's body, avoiding looking in the eye, frequent arm and leg movement, leg crossing, and voice fluctuations (quick/slow), etc.

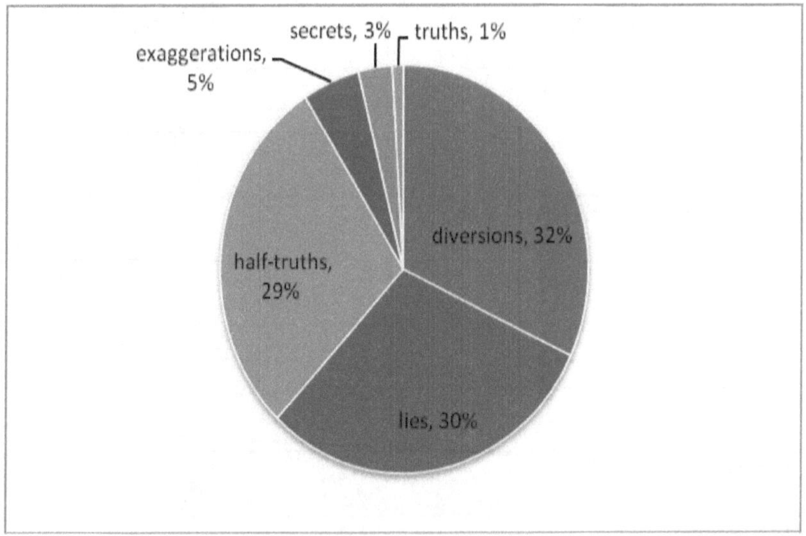

Figure 7.1 Share of truths and lies in communication

Chiru also presents a study by De Paulo, Lanieir and Davis (1983, in Chiru, 2009) who, based on experiments, suggested a grid containing possible indices in lying people and frequency of lies (Table 7.1).

Table 7.1. Possible indices of lie and frequency of lies (after De Paulo, Lanieir and Davis, 1983, in Chiru, 2009, 172-173)

Indices of lie	Frequency of lie
Hand to head	12-1
Vague answer	10-1
Self-contact or play with close objects	8-1
Interruption	6-1
Look at the watch	5-1
Hesitation	5-1
Weak visual contact	4-1
Mouth dryness	3-1
Withdrawal of legs under the chair	3-1
Arm crossing	3-1
Tapping the table with the fingers	2-1

We can easily see that the probability of detecting a lie in computer-mediated communication and, implicitly, in virtual communication – be it sms, chat, e-mail, socialisation network – is low because this type of communication is done through technological means of communication: hence, the risk of such communication for those who do not alternate virtual communication and face-to-face communication or, at least, with image transfer (Skype).

7.2 Communication and Manipulation

Below are a few additions to the risks of manipulating ("1. managing or influencing skilfully, especially in an unfair manner: 'to manipulate people's feelings'; 2. handling, managing, or using, especially with skill, in some process of treatment or performance: 'to manipulate a large tractor'." – *manipulate. Dictionary.com Unabridged.* Online: http://dictionary.reference.com/browse/manipulating) or of being manipulated through virtual communication.

Words have power, importance, and meaning (Tripp, 2013, 17). This reality shows the influence of our words on the other communication partners. Words can be used both positively (to encourage, inform, etc.), and negatively (to manipulate, for instance).

This should not make us not argue. Since there is potential risk, we should not give up arguing, but we need to give up subversive techniques. Many honest people refuse to prepare an argument because doing it, taking interest in the other, trying to understand the other would mean practicing some kind of "rape of consciousness" or, in a less dramatic way, "not minding their own business" (Breton, 2009, 61).

Another form of argumentation is persuasion, "a way of convincing and influencing individual and group behaviours and attitudes." (Zanc, 2005, 120) persuasion is a higher pressure exerted during the process of argumentation.

Manipulation is doubled by selfish intents (be they personal or group intents) and use techniques of argumentation or persuasion to reach these hidden goals and make the receiver act accordingly.

The fear of manipulating or of not being manipulated can weaken the social link; it can create social distance right in the fields where communication should lead to discussion, mutual knowledge and share.

Words, be they uttered, written or transmitted through technological means, have the power to manipulate. The more intense and quick communication is, the greater the risk of being caught off guard in manipulative communication. Sometimes, our brain may find it difficult to process the huge amount of communication per time unit. This can lead to major psychical and spiritual unbalance. According to a study carried out by the European Commission, in 2020, depression will be the disease with the highest incidence in the world.

We should not hide the fact that language is sometimes used to lie, to mask certain realities, to persuade people and to manipulate masses." (Slama-Cazacu, 2000, 50)

Efficient communication is not always impossible. But it always confronts with noise, bad intent, manipulation techniques, and deviant behaviour people. This should raise our awareness and make us avoid such senders and being deceived as receivers. Knowing the foundations of communication – traps, obstacles and invisible stakes – allows higher efficiency in communication (Cabin and Dortier, 2010, 20).

Conclusions

Communication is ubiquitous in social processes and we have to deal with it on a daily basis. This is due to man's need for interacting with his peers.

Communication types are varied, but we only tackled in this book verbal communication, non-verbal communication and computer-mediated communication (a sub-type of verbal communication). I have tried to approach this type of communication and my conclusion is that computer-mediated communication observes widely accepted communication schemes but, compared to face-to-face communication, it is less efficient, less safe and less fulfilling: computer-mediated communication is a completion to other types of communication if we manage to put aside the risks of mediated communication.

"Efficient communication needs a lot of work in a certain order: to want to communicate, to have something to say and then to find the best ways to do it." (Ritt, 2004, 189)

Communication shapes all our relationships: from our relationship with God to our relationships with our families, children, and colleagues.

At the same time, we took into account the risks of virtual communication but we do not believe technophobia can solve the problem: virtual communication exists and it should be taken as such and seen as a form of sometimes dangerous imperfect communication; it should not replace face-to-face communication – the most complex and efficient type of communication. Media devices cannot replace a subject who thinks, imagines, communicates and desires, a subject that existed before and independently of these bloody means of communication, a subject that used to be self-confident, vigilant, and free from any kind of alienation (Bougnoux, 2000, 74).

Some authors claim there is no life without communication. Maybe this is true, maybe not. What is certain is that without communication we would be poorer, sadder, and lonelier.

On the other hand, we need to be able to manage communication acts to avoid tension: we need to deepen them, to fulfil them and to improve them.

References

Adler, Mortimer J. (1982). *The Angels and Us.* New York, NY: Macmillan Publishing Company, Inc.

Agabrian, Mircea. (2008). *Strategii de comunicare eficientă.* Iaşi: Institutul European.

Albu, Gabriel. (2008). *Comunicarea interpersonală.* Iaşi: Institutul European.

Alman, S., Valenzi, E. and Hodgetts, R. (1985). *Organizational Behavior: Theory and Practice.* Orlando, FL: Academic Press.

Amado, Gilles and Guittet, André. (2007). *Psihologia comunicării în grupuri.* Iaşi: Editura Polirom.

Argyle, Michael and Henderson, Monika. (1985). *The Anatomy of Relationship: And the Rules and Skills Needed to Handle Them Successfully.* London: Penguin Books.

Baran, Stanley J. and David, Dennis K. (2000). *Mass Communication Theory. Foundation, Ferment, and Future.* Belmont, CA: Wadsworth.

Barriers to Communication. Online: http://www.businessdictionary.com/definition/barriers-to-communication.html.

Barton, Bruce. (2008). Subjectivity, Culture, Communications, Intermedia: A Meditation on the "Impure Interactions" of Performance and the "In-between" Space of Intimacy in a Wired World. *Theatre Research in Canada 29 (1):* 51-92.

Beciu, Camelia. (2011). *Sociologia comunicării şi a spaţiului public.* Iaşi: Editura Polirom.

Beldad, Ardion, de Jong, Menno and Steehouder, Michael. (2011). A Comprehensive Theoretical Framework for Personal Information-Related Behaviours on the Internet. *The Information Society 27*: 220-232.

Biberi, Ion. (1972). *Arta de a scrie şi de a vorbi în public.* Bucureşti: Editura Enciclopedică Română.

Biblia sau *Sfânta Scriptură a Vechiului şi Noului Testament.* (1995). Translated by D. Cornilescu, United Bible Societies.

Breton, Philippe. (2009). *Convinge fără să manipulezi.* Iaşi: Institutul European.

Bougnoux, Daniel. (2000). *Introducere în ştiinţele comunicării.* Iaşi: Editura Polirom.

Cabin. Philippe and Dortier, Jean-François. (Eds.). (2010). *Comunicarea. Perspective actuale.* Iaşi: Editura Polirom.

Cameron, Milton. (2005). *Comunicarea prin gesturi şi atitudini. Cum să înveţi limbajul trupului.* Iaşi: Editura Polirom.

Chiru, Irena. (2009). *Comunicarea interpersonală.* Bucureşti: Editura Tritonic.

Cojocaru, Oleg. *Adobe a publicat lista celor mai mari retele de socializare pe Internet.* Online: http://incomemagazine.ro/articole/adobe-a-publicat-lista-celor-mai-mari-retele-de-socializare-pe-internet.

Cristescu, G., Roman, R., Horvath, T., Barbonţa, L. and Borzak, T. (1999). *Comunicarea profesională*. Timişoara: Editura Mirton.

Dance, Frank E. X. (1970). The concept of communication. *The Journal of Communication 20*: 201-210.

Daniels, Tom D. and Spiker, Barry K. (1987). *Perspectives on Organizational Communication*. Dubuque, IO: WM.C. Brown Publishers.

Descamps, Marc-Alain. (1989). *Le langage du corps et la communication corporelle*. Paris: Presses Universitaires de France.

DeVito, Joseph A., (1986). *The Communication Handbook: A Dictionary*. New York, NY: Harper & Row.

Dignen, Bob. *Teaching virtual communication skills*. Online: http://peo.cambridge.org/index.php?option=com_content&view=arti cle&id=189:teaching-virtual-communication-skills-by-bob-dignan&catid=3:blog&Itemid=2.

Dinu, Mihai. (2000). *Comunicarea: Repere fundamentale*. Bucureşti: Editura Algos.

Dinu, Mihai. (2004). *Fundamentele comunicării interpersonale*. Bucureşti: Editura Bic All.

Dobson, James. (2012). *Fetele – cum să le creştem. Sfaturi practice şi încurajări pentru cei ce modelează viitoarea generaţie de femei*. Oradea: Editura Imago Dei.

Drăgan, Ioan. (2007). *Comunicarea: Paradigme şi teorii*. Bucureşti: Editura RAO.

Drăgan, Ion. (1980). *Opinia publică, comunicarea de masă şi propaganda*. Bucureşti: Editura Ştiinţifică şi Enciclopedică.

Eibl-Eibesfeldt, Irenäus. (1998). *Iubire şi ură*. Bucureşti: Editura Trei.

Facebook. Online: http://en.wikipedia.org/wiki/Facebook.

Facebook: 10 years of social networking, in numbers. Online: http://www.theguardian.com/news/datablog/2014/feb/04/facebook-in-numbers-statistics.

Fârte, Gheorghe-Ilie. (2004). *Comunicarea: O abordare praxiologică*. Iaşi: Casa Editorială Demiurg.

Fiske, John. (2003). *Introducere în ştiinţele comunicării*. Iaşi: Editura Polirom.

Fizeşan, Bianca. (2010). (Re)construction of Identity in the Virtual Space of Second Life. *Revista de informatică socială III (13)*: 43-61.

Floyd, Kory. (2013). *Comunicarea interpersonală*. Iaşi: Editura Polirom.

Forsyth, Donelson R. (1983). *An Introduction to Group Dynamics*. Pacific Grove, CA: Brooks/Cole Publishing Company.

Haineş, Ion. (1998). *Introducere în teoria comunicării*. Bucureşti: Editura Fundaţiei "România de Mâine".

Hartley, Mary. (2005). *Limbajul trupului la serviciu*. Iaşi: Editura Polirom.

Hendrick, Clyde and Hendrick, Susan S. (1986). Lovers wear rose coloured glasses. *Journal of Social and Personal Relationships 5*: 161-183.

Intimacy. Dictionary.com Unabridged. Online: http://dictionary.reference.com/browse/intimacy.

Lemeni, Adrian. *Cultura virtuală – expresie a unei false comunicări.* Online: http://www.crestinortodox.ro/religie/cultura-virtuala-expresie-unei-false-comunicari-118483.html.

Lie. Dictionary.com Unabridged. Online: http://dictionary.reference.com/browse/lie

Lohisse, Jean. (2002). *Comunicarea: De la transmiterea mecanică la interacţiune.* Iaşi: Editura Polirom.

Macrae, Fiona. *Sorry to interrupt, dear, but women really do talk more than men (13,000 words a day more to be precise).* Online: http://www.dailymail.co.uk/sciencetech/article-2281891/Women-really-talk-men-13-000-words-day-precise.html.

Manipulate. Dictionary.com Unabridged. Online: http://dictionary.reference.com/browse/manipulate.

Maslow, A. (1943). A Theory of Human Motivation. *Psychological Review 50*: 370-396.

Maslow's Hierarchy of Needs. Online: http://en.wikipedia.org/wiki/Maslow%27s_hierarchy_of_needs#mediaviewer/File:MaslowsHierarchyOfNeeds.svg.

McQuail, Denis. (1999). *Comunicarea.* Iaşi: Institutul European.

Mitrofan, Nicolae. (1984). *Dragostea şi căsătoria.* Bucureşti: Editura Ştiinţifică şi Enciclopedică.

Moles, Abraham A. (1974). *Sociodinamica culturii.* Bucureşti: Editura Ştiinţifică.

Müller, Marion G. (2008). Visual competence: a new paradigm for studying visuals in the social sciences? *Visual Studies 23 (2)*: 101-112.

Muntean, Ana. (2006). *Psihologia dezvoltării umane*. Iaşi: Editura Polirom.

Nadolu, Bogdan. (2007). *Sociologia comunicării de masă*. Timişoara: Editura Excelsior Art.

Neagoe, Alexandru. (2007). *Asistenţa socială a familiei: O abordare sistemică*. Timişoara: Editura Universităţii de Vest.

Neagoe, Alexandru. (Ed.). (2011). *Values and Spirituality in Social Work Practice*. Bonn: Verlag fur Kultur und Wissenschaft.

Nevoia de spiritualitate. Online: http://adevarul.ro/international/in-lume/nevoia-spiritualitate-1_50ba02a77c42d5a663afa38f/index.html.

Noica, Constantin. (1996). *Cuvânt împreună despre rostirea românească*. Bucureşti: Editura Humanitas.

Non-verbal Communication. Online: http://www.businessdictionary.com/definition/non-verbal-communication.html#ixzz3Ndv4JQJV.

Nuţă, Adrian. (2004). *Abilităţi de comunicare*. Bucureşti: Editura Sper.

Ognev, Ivan and Russev, Vladimir. (2005). *Securitatea psihologică*. Bucureşti: Editura Fundaţiei Culturale "Ideea Europeană".

O'Sullivan, Tim, Hartley, John, Saunders, Danny, Mongomery, Martin and Fishe, John. (2001). *Concepte fundamentale din ştiinţele comunicării şi studiile culturale*. Iaşi: Editura Polirom.

Otovescu, Adrian. (Ed.). (2012). *Sociologia comunicării: perspective teoretice şi cercetări de teren*. Bucureşti: Editura Pro Universitaria.

Papa, Nicole. *Effective Virtual Communication*. Online: http://www.ehow.com/about_6756180_effective-virtualcommunication.html#page=0.

Pânişoară, Ion-Ovidiu. (2008). *Comunicarea eficientă*. Iaşi: Editura Polirom.

Perry, B. D. (2002). Childhood Experience and the Expression of Genetic Potential: What Childhood Neglect Tells Us about Nature and Nurture. *Brain and Mind 3 (1)*: 79-100.

Raţă, Georgeta. (2001). *Contribuţii la teoria comunicării*. Timişoara: Editura Mirton.

Răşcanu, Ruxandra. (2007). *Psihologie şi comunicare*. Bucureşti: Editura Universităţii din Bucureşti.

Rich, Hilary and Kravitz, Helaina Laks. (2006). *Căsnicia perfectă: Sfaturi şi secrete pentru cei căsătoriţi, indiferent de vârstă*. Bucureşti: Editura Teora.

Ritt, Adriana. (2004). *Introducere în comunicare*. Timişoara: Editura Mirton.

Sachelarie, Octavian Mihai and Petrescu, Victor. (2006). *Sociologia comunicării*. Piteşti: Editura Paralela 45.

Shannon, Claude E. and Weaver, Warren. (1949). *The Mathematical Theory of Communication*. Champaign, IL: University of Illinois Press.

Silvaş, Alexandra and Modrea, Arina. (2012). Bariere în procesul de comunicare. *Proceedings of the International Conference "Communication, context, interdisciplinarity" 2*: 250-254.

Slama-Cazacu, Tatiana. (2000). *Stratageme comunicaţionale şi manipularea*. Iaşi: Editura Polirom.

Şerb, Stancu. (2007). *Relaţii publice şi comunicare*. Bucureşti: Editura Teora.

Şoitu, Laurenţiu. (2001). *Pedagogia comunicării*. Iaşi: Institutul European.

Ştefănescu, Simona. (2009). *Sociologia comunicării*. Tîrgovişte: Editura Cetatea de Scaun.

The American Heritage Dictionary of the English Language. Online: http://www.yourdictionary.com/virtual#americanheritage.

The most popular social networking sites by country. Online: http://en.wikipedia.org/wiki/Facebook#mediaviewer/File:Social_net works.jpg

Tisseron, Serge. (2013). *Lumea virtuală: avataruri şi fantome*. Bucureşti: Editura Trei.

Tran, Vasile and Stănciugelu, Irina. (2003). *Teoria comunicării*. Bucureşti: Editura Comunicare.ro.

Tripp, Paul David. (2013). *Războiul vorbelor. Abordarea problemelor de comunicare*. Oradea: Editura Scriptum.

Truth. Dictionary.com Unabridged. Online: http://dictionary.reference.com/browse/truth).

Vaghin, Igor and Gluschai, Antonina. (2006). *Manipularea erotică*. Bucureşti: Editura Fundaţiei Culturale "Ideea Europeană".

Van Cuilenburg, J. J., Scholten, O. and Noomen, G. W. (1998). *Ştiinţa comunicării*. Bucureşti: Editura Humanitas.

Verbal Communication. Online: http://www.businessdictionary.com/definition/verbal-communication.html#ixzz3NdtXjVo5.

Voinea, Mihai, Delcea, Cristian and Varninschi, Alex. *Efectele Facebook. Cum am ajuns să ne spionăm între noi şi ce spune SRI despre monitorizarea reţelelor sociale*. Online: http://adevarul.ro/tech/retele-sociale/video-efectele-facebook-ajuns-spionam-spune-sri-despre-monitorizarea-retelelor-sociale1_53971dd80d133766a875783a/index.html.

Watzlawick, Paul, Beavin-Bavelas, Janet and Jackson, Don. (1967). *Pragmatics of Human Communication: A Study of Interactional Patterns, Pathologies and Paradoxes*. New York, NY: W. W. Norton.

Werner, Severin and Tankard, James. (2004). *Perspective asupra comunicării de masă*. Iaşi: Editura Polirom.

Willard, Dallas. (1990). *În cautarea călăuzirii. Dezvoltarea unei relaţii conversaţionale cu Dumnezeu*. Oradea: Editura Cartea Creştină.

Yeung, K. T. and Martin, J. L. (2003). The Looking Glass Self: An Empirical Test and Elaboration. *Social Forces 81*: 843-879.

Zamfir, Cătălin and Vlăsceanu, Lazăr. (Eds.). (1998). *Dicţionar de sociologie*. Bucureşti: Editura Babel.

Zanc, Ioan. (2005). *Informaţie şi comunicare*. Cluj-Napoca: Editura Dacia.

www.ingramcontent.com/pod-product-compliance
Lightning Source LLC
Chambersburg PA
CBHW031243250726
48655CB00005B/2059